Windows Vista explained

Books Available

By the same authors:

BP585	Microsoft Excel 2007 explained
BP584	Microsoft Word 2007 explained
BP583	Microsoft Office 2007 explained
BP581	Windows Vista explained
BP580	Windows Vista for Beginners
BP569	Microsoft Works 8 and Works Suite 2006 explained
BP563	Using Windows XP's accessories
BP558	Microsoft Works 8.0 & Works Suite 2005 explained
BP557	How Did I Do That ... in Windows XP
BP555	Using PDF Files
BP550	Advanced Guide to Windows XP
BP548	Easy PC Keyboard Shortcuts
BP545	Paint Shop Pro 8 explained
BP544	Microsoft Office 2003 explained
BP538	Windows XP for Beginners
BP525	Controlling Windows XP the easy way
BP514	Windows XP explained
BP513	IE 6 and Outlook Express 6 explained
BP512	Microsoft Access 2002 explained
BP511	Microsoft Excel 2002 explained
BP510	Microsoft Word 2002 explained
BP509	Microsoft Office XP explained
BP498	Using Visual Basic
BP487	Quicken 2000 UK explained
BP486	Using Linux the easy way
BP465	Lotus SmartSuite Millennium explained
BP433	Your own Web site on the Internet
BP341	MS-DOS explained
BP284	Programming in QuickBASIC
BP258	Learning to Program in C

Windows Vista explained

by

N. Kantaris

and

P.R.M. Oliver

Bernard Babani (publishing) Ltd
The Grampians
Shepherds Bush Road
London W6 7NF
England

www.babanibooks.com

Please Note

Although every care has been taken with the production of this book to ensure that any projects, designs, modifications and/or programs, etc., contained herewith, operate in a correct and safe manner and also that any components specified are normally available in Great Britain, the Publishers and Author(s) do not accept responsibility in any way for the failure (including fault in design) of any project, design, modification or program to work correctly or to cause damage to any equipment that it may be connected to or used in conjunction with, or in respect of any other damage or injury that may be so caused, nor do the Publishers accept responsibility in any way for the failure to obtain specified components.

Notice is also given that if equipment that is still under warranty is modified in any way or used or connected with home-built equipment then that warranty may be void.

© 2007 BERNARD BABANI (publishing) LTD

First Published – June 2007

British Library Cataloguing in Publication Data:

A catalogue record for this book is available from the British Library

ISBN 978 0 85934 581 1

Cover Design by Gregor Arthur
Printed and Bound in Great Britain by Cox & Wyman Ltd., Reading.

The Windows History

The first version of Windows was produced by Microsoft in 1983 as a graphical extension to its Disc Operating System (MS-DOS). This, however, was not successful because, being DOS based, it was confined to the DOS memory limit of 1 MB of RAM – rather a lot of memory at that time!

In 1987, an Intel 386 processor specific version of Windows was launched that was able to run in multiple 'virtual 8086' mode, but Windows applications were still unable to use any extended memory above the 1 MB. In 1990, however, Windows version 3.0 solved this problem and became a huge success.

Two years later, the much needed update, Windows 3.1, was released to fix most of the program bugs in version 3.0. The horrendous and frequent 'Unrecoverable Application Error' message became a thing of the past (almost!). Windows for Workgroups 3.1, followed in October 1992, and started to give the program the power to control small networked groups of computers. This was strengthened in October 1993 with the 3.11 release, which included 32-bit file management and more networking support.

Then, three years later, came Windows 95, a 32-bit operating system in its own right which made full use of the 32-bit features of the then available range of Intel processor chips. Microsoft had also put a lot of effort into this system to make it compatible with almost all existing Windows and MS-DOS based applications. This was obviously necessary, but It meant that parts of Windows 95 were still only 16-bit in operation.

In June 1998, Microsoft launched Windows 98 which ran faster, crashed less frequently, supported a host of new technologies, such as DVD for storing digital video, and improved MMX multimedia. In May 1999 Windows 98 Second Edition was released.

In September 2000, Microsoft released Windows Me, as the direct upgrade to Windows 95/98 for the home PC. Windows Me loaded faster, run more reliably, and if things went radically wrong, it had the ability to return to a previous working version of the Operating System. In addition, Windows Me incorporated Wizards that let you set up home networks and gave you the ability to share Internet connections, had improved support for digital cameras, video recorders, and multimedia with the introduction of the Windows Media Player 7. Also, improved features and tools in Internet Explorer 5.5 allowed better Web communication from e-mail to instant messaging to video conferencing.

Running parallel with the desktop Windows development, Microsoft set up in 1989 the Windows NT development team. Its mission was to design and build an operating system, primarily for the business server community, which was robust and extensible. In October 1991, the first version of Windows NT was shown to the public at COMDEX – the world's largest PC exhibition.

In August 1993, Windows NT 3.1 was released, followed a year later by Windows NT 3.5. In June 1995 Windows NT 3.51 was released capable of supporting upcoming Windows 95 programs. Then, in August 1996 Microsoft released Windows NT 4.0. Since then, much has changed with Windows NT 4.0, as customer requirements evolved to include support for Windows applications, Web services, communications, and much more. These improvements came in the guise of several Service Packs.

In February 2000, Microsoft released Windows 2000 Professional, together with two additional Windows NT compatible versions of the software; Server and Advanced Server. Users of Windows 95/98 could easily upgrade to the Windows 2000 Professional version of this Operating System (OS), while users of Windows NT could upgrade to one of the other two versions of the OS. In October 2001, Microsoft released Windows XP (XP for eXPerience) in two flavours; the Home edition (less expensive) as the direct upgrade to Windows 98/Me for home users and the Professional edition (more expensive but with additional functionality) for Windows 2000 or business users. Of course, provided you were running Windows 98/Me or Windows 2000, you could upgrade to either version of Windows XP.

Windows XP looked slightly different to previous versions of Windows – there were changes to the desktop icons, start menu and the Control Panel, while other concepts were borrowed from Windows Me or Windows 2000.

Windows XP had many improvements incorporated into it, such as added features that made it load faster than any previous version of Windows, run more reliably, and the ability to return to a previous working version of the Operating System, improved Wizards to let you set up home networks a lot easier and give you the ability to share Internet connections, improved support for digital cameras, video recorders, and multimedia with an improved version of the Windows Media Player (version 9), improved features and tools in Internet Explorer 6 which allowed faster performance, and better Web communication from e-mail (using version 6 of Outlook Express) to instant messaging to video conferencing using the MSN Explorer, and improved Windows File Protection which prevented the replacement of protected system and executable files.

Following the launch of Windows XP in 2001, there followed two major updates in the form of Service Pack 1 (SP1) and, in August 2004, Service Pack 2 (SP2). The latter update focused mainly on security of the computer, and was over 260 MB in size. Microsoft made security the central theme of SP2, although there were some additional features that were not specifically geared to protecting your computer. The main visible changes were to be seen in the form of additional Control Panel utilities which allowed the automatic access of a new Security Centre which monitored a PC's security settings with respect to its Firewall, Automatic Updates, and Virus protection. In addition SP2 protected areas of memory where previously viruses could hide and execute without one's knowledge.

Finally, in February 2006, Microsoft launched the long awaited Windows Vista. This release of Windows comes in several versions, as explained at the beginning of Chapter 1, and is more than an Operating System. Vista comes with software that allow you to browse the Web, send and receive e-mail messages, burn CDs and DVDs, edit photos and videos, and home entertainment. It also comes with a range of security tools, although you will need to buy anti-virus protection. Vista is by far the most complete Windows release to date.

About this Book

Windows Vista explained was written to help people who recently bought a computer with any one of the four available versions of the Vista operating system. The most frequent question which comes to mind is "having bought the computer, what can I do with it now?"

Answers might include; keeping in touch with your children or grandchildren, browsing the Internet to get some useful information, downloading the photographs from your digital camera and storing them on the computer's hard disc, or simply getting to grips with simple word processing, or running educational programs for your offspring. The choice is endless.

Whatever your reasons for buying a computer, it is very important to understand its operating system (in this case Windows Vista), because it is the operating system that allows you to run other programs, store and retrieve information, and looks after the health of your PC.

The material in this book is presented using simple language, avoiding jargon as much as possible, but with such a subject some is inevitable, so a short glossary of terms is included, which should be used with the text of this book, where necessary, for an explanation of the most obscure definitions.

The book is structured on the 'what you need to know first, appears first' basis, although you don't have to start at the beginning and go right through to the end, as the chapters have been designed to be fairly self-contained. We even cover the Windows Vista security utilities which allow you to automatically update Windows Vista, and monitor your PC's settings with respect to its Firewall, and Virus protection.

The present book was written with the non technical, non computer literate person in mind. It is hoped that with its help you will be able to get the most out of your computer, when using Windows Vista, and that you will be able to do it in the shortest, most effective and enjoyable way. Have fun!

About the Authors

Noel Kantaris graduated in Electrical Engineering at Bristol University and after spending three years in the Electronics Industry in London, took up a Tutorship in Physics at the University of Queensland. Research interests in Ionospheric Physics, led to the degrees of M.E. in Electronics and Ph.D. in Physics. On return to the UK, he took up a Post-Doctoral Research Fellowship in Radio Physics at the University of Leicester, and then a lecturing position in Engineering at the Camborne School of Mines, Cornwall, (part of Exeter University), where he was also the CSM Computing Manager. At present he is IT Director of FFC Ltd.

Phil Oliver graduated in Mining Engineering at Camborne School of Mines and has specialised in most aspects of surface mining technology, with a particular emphasis on computer related techniques. He has worked in Guyana, Canada, several Middle Eastern and Central Asian countries, South Africa and the United Kingdom, on such diverse projects as: the planning and management of bauxite, iron, gold and coal mines; rock excavation contracting in the UK; international mining equipment sales and international mine consulting. He later took up a lecturing position at Camborne School of Mines (part of Exeter University) in Surface Mining and Management. He has now retired, to spend more time writing, consulting, and developing Web sites.

Acknowledgements

We would like to thank friends and colleagues, for their helpful tips and suggestions which assisted us in the writing of this book.

Trademarks

HP and **LaserJet** are registered trademarks of Hewlett Packard Corporation.

Microsoft, **Windows**, **Windows XP**, and **Windows Vista** are either registered trademarks or trademarks of Microsoft Corporation.

PostScript is a registered trademark of Adobe Systems Incorporated.

All other brand and product names used in the book are recognised as trademarks, or registered trademarks, of their respective companies.

Contents

1

Installing Windows Vista

Windows Vista is available in four editions: The Home Basic (less expensive) and suitable for existing PCs; the Home Premium edition (more expensive, but with additional features, such as the Aero desktop experience and 3D graphics, has more options for collaborating with other users, supports the Media Center, and has added security and simplified management); the Business edition which substitutes business networking and hardware protection for the Media Centre facility; and the Ultimate edition which includes everything.

Although we have used the Windows Ultimate edition to write this book, we will only cover what is common with the Windows Home Premium edition, as most home PC users will find that these common options between the two editions contain all the facilities they will ever need.

In Windows Vista, Microsoft has adopted Explorer type shells which are customised to display specific file types, such as media, pictures, music and video. The Explorer displays a preview of the selected item at the bottom part of the window and the toolbar displays command actions specific to the selected file type. We will examine the Explorer windows in more detail later on.

In what follows in this chapter we discuss what hardware you need for the different versions of Windows Vista, what you need to know prior to installing it, and how to install it whether you choose to upgrade or make a clean install.

If you have bought a computer with Windows Vista already installed, then you could easily skip the rest of this chapter.

If, however, you are upgrading your computer's operating system from a previous version of Windows to Windows Vista and want to know what preparations you need to make to your system, and how to transfer your various settings, then read on.

The Vista Editions

Windows Vista comes in four editions; Home Basic, Home Premium, Business, and Ultimate. Each of these editions supports slightly different requirements, designed by Microsoft to enhance the experience of every kind of PC user. These, as listed in Microsoft's Web site, are as follows:

Features	Home Basic	Home Premium	Business	Ultimate
Security with Windows Defender and Windows Firewall	✓	✓	✓	✓
Find what you need with Instant Search and Internet Explorer 7	✓	✓	✓	✓
Aero Desktop and 3D Experience		✓	✓	✓
Mobility Support		✓	✓	✓
Collaborate and Share Documents		✓	✓	✓
Photos and Media Center		✓		✓
Business Backup			✓	✓
Business Networking			✓	✓
Data protection				✓

Table 1.1 Windows Vista Editions.

As can be seen from Table 1.1, Windows Home Basic is for upgrading existing PCs to Windows Vista without any additional hardware requirements – such computers are designated as Windows Vista Capable PCs, while to run the other three editions and get the maximum Vista experience, you might need to buy new hardware or even a new computer – designated as Windows Vista Premium Ready PCs.

A Windows Vista Capable PC requires:

A modern processor with a speed of at least 800 MHz, 512 MB of system memory (RAM), and a graphics processor that is DirectX 9 capable.

A Windows Vista Premium Ready PC requires:

A processor with a speed of at least 1 GHz 32-bit (x86) or 64-bit (x64), 1 GB of system memory (RAM), a graphics processor that is DirectX 9 capable with a WDDM driver and at least 128 MB of dedicated graphics memory, 40 GB of hard drive capacity with 15 GB free space, a DVD-ROM drive, audio output capability, and Internet access.

In addition, other features of Vista, such as the ability to watch and record live TV, will require suitable hardware such as a TV tuner with remote control and a HD (High Definition) DVD drive.

If you intend to buy a new Windows Vista Premium Ready laptop, make sure that apart from the other requirements listed above it is also equipped with a hybrid hard disc, which is a hard disc with built-in flash memory that helps reduce power consumption and extends battery life.

Essential Tasks Prior to Installing Vista

Before installing or upgrading to Windows Vista, you need to complete two tasks: (a) run Windows Update, and (b) select which version of Windows Vista is most suitable for your PC.

To run Windows Update, click on the **Start** button, then point to **All Programs** and click on the **Windows Update** option on the displayed menu, as shown in Fig. 1.1.

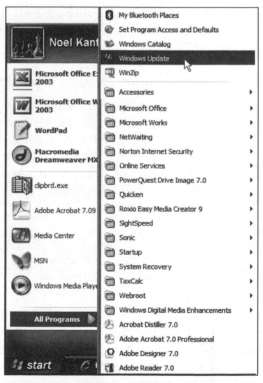

Fig. 1.1 Selecting the Windows Update.

This opens the **Windows Update** in an Internet Explorer window (you must be connected to the Internet for this to work), as shown in Fig. 1.2 on the next page.

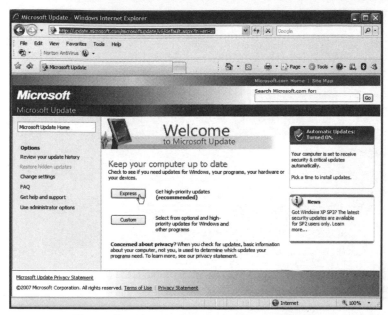

Fig. 1.2 Starting the Windows Express Update.

Click on the **Express** button to download and install all the required updates. Once this is completed, you are ready to connect to the Microsoft Web site to select the best version of Windows Vista for your PC, whether you have already bought one or not, as the upgrade advisor also tests your PC's peripherals and installed programs.

To do so, start the Internet Explorer and type

Http://www.microsoft.com/windows/products/windowsvista/ buyorupgrade/upgradeadvisor.mspx

in its address bar (all in one line and without any breaks).

This should open the Advisor screen, shown in Fig. 1.3 on the next page, unless Microsoft has changed the position of the Upgrade Advisor on its Web site, in which case you will have to follows appropriate links starting from the Microsoft Home page.

Fig. 1.3 Downloading the Windows Upgrade Advisor.

As you can see from the displayed Advisor screen, you should plug into your PC all the peripherals, such as printers, scanner, and any other USB devices. Next, scroll down the screen and click the **Download Windows Vista Upgrade Advisor** link, and on the displayed screen click the **Download** button. In following screens install and run the Advisor – just follow the advice on the displayed screens.

Eventually the Welcome to Windows Vista Upgrade Advisor screen will display on which you should click the **Start Scan** button. A few moments later the scan is completed and you can see in the report a recommendation on the Vista version most suited to your PC, and details on System, Device, and Program compatibility. There is also a **Task List** which you should print out and follow to the letter before and after installing Windows Vista.

Upgrading to Windows Vista

Windows Vista is sold as either a 32-bit Operating System (OS), or a 64-bit OS. Naturally, for the 64-bit OS you will require a 64-bit computer, so be careful.

To upgrade to Windows Vista, your computer must be running Windows XP Service Pack 2 (SP2) and, of course, it must be capable of actually running one of the Windows Vista editions. Even then, you'll have to decide whether to:

a. Upgrade, which replaces Windows XP with Windows Vista and retains all your settings, data files, and programs, or

b. Back-up your settings and data files, and then go for a clean install, thus eliminating the gradual slowdown that tends to happen to frequently used PCs over time. This method also has the advantage of cleaning your PC of any bugs it might have acquired from the Internet. However, the downside is that you'll have to reinstall all your favourite programs.

If your current PC is running earlier versions of Windows, but is capable of running Windows Vista, then you will need to make a new (clean) installation of Windows Vista, in which case you will have to make a back-up of all your data files, but you'll lose all your settings and you will also have to reinstall all your programs from scratch.

Luckily for users of Windows XP, Windows Vista includes a program in its distribution DVD, called Windows Easy Transfer, which can help you transfer your settings and data files from your old computer to your new computer. But first, you must Install Windows Vista on your new computer, then run Windows Easy Transfer on it, before running it on your old computer.

Installing Windows Vista

To start the installation process, switch on your PC, start Windows, and insert the Windows Vista distribution DVD into the DVD drive. After a few seconds the **Setup** program will run automatically from the DVD.

If the **Setup** program does not run automatically, click the **Start** button and in the Start Search box (just above it), and shown in Fig. 1.4 below, type 'Run' (without the quotation marks) and press the **Enter** key.

Fig. 1.4 The Windows Vista Start Search Box.

This opens the Run dialogue box, shown in Fig. 1.5, in the **Open** box of which you type **E:\setup**, where **E:** is the letter that represents our DVD drive (yours might be different), and click the **OK** button.

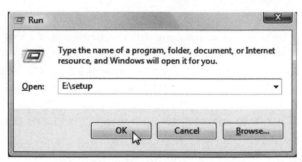

Fig. 1.5 The Run Dialogue Screen.

The **Setup** program then displays the screen shown in Fig. 1.6 on the next page.

Fig. 1.6 The Windows Vista Installation Screen.

Clicking the **Install now** button, starts the installation of Windows. On the next three screens, you are asked to go online to get the latest update for the **Setup** program, then enter the product key, followed by your acceptance of the licence terms. Next, the screen shown in Fig. 1.7 is displayed.

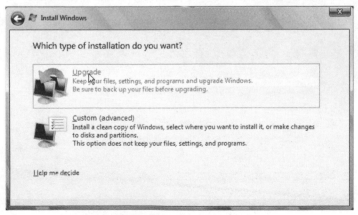

Fig. 1.7 The Install Windows Screen.

On the Install Windows screen you are asked to specify the type of installation you prefer, 'Upgrade' or 'Custom'.

As the computer we were installing Windows Vista was less than a month old, we chose the 'Upgrade' option. This displayed a 'Compatibility Report' listing all the potential issues detected by **Setup** with installed applications or devices, which should be noted so as to try to deal with them later. Next, Windows starts copying files, etc., and it restarts automatically a few times.

Warning: If your computer is configured to start from a CD or DVD, <u>don't</u> press any keyboard key if asked to on a Windows restart – just allow Windows to restart by itself, not forcing it to start from the CD or DVD. If you interfere, you might have to roll back to the previous version of Windows and start the installation process all over again from the beginning!

The final screen is the 'Date and Time' display, after which you are asked to click a **Start** button to start Windows Vista which displayed the screen in Fig. 1.8.

Fig. 1.8 The Windows Vista Welcome Center.

The type of installation we selected took around 90 minutes to complete. Although it is said that this is the longest installation, we did not have to reinstall all our program applications, or our settings.

Starting the Windows Easy Transfer Utility

The **Windows Easy Transfer** utility program is available on the Windows Vista installation DVD. You should start this program on your <u>new</u> computer first after installing Windows Vista. To do so, switch on your computer, start Windows Vista, and insert the Windows Vista distribution DVD in the DVD drive. After a few seconds the **Setup** program will run automatically from the DVD, displaying the screen in Fig. 1.9.

Fig. 1.9 The Starting Screen of the Easy Transfer Utility.

Next, click the **Transfer files and settings from another computer** link pointed to in the above screen. The program then prepares to run, and after a few seconds displays the screen shown in Fig. 1.10 on the next page.

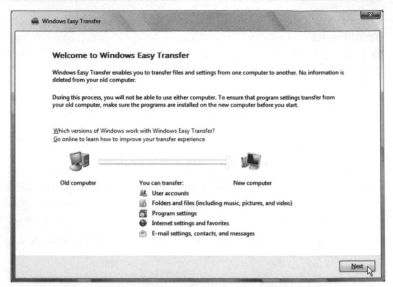

Fig. 1.10 The Welcome Screen of the Easy Transfer Utility.

Note that only if your old computer is running Windows XP can you transfer your User Accounts, Program Settings, Internet Settings with Favorites, and E-mail Settings with your Contacts and Messages.

If, however, you old computer is running Windows 2000, then you can only use the **Windows Easy Transfer** program to transfer your data files, but not the rest. With earlier versions of Windows, all you can do is copy your data on CD or DVD or an external portable hard disc, then transfer them manually into the appropriate folders in Window Vista.

In the next screen of the **Windows Easy Transfer** program you are asked to tell the program whether this is your new or old computer, whether you have the special Easy Transfer cable connecting the two computers, or you want to use other media, such as a stack of CDs, a few DVDs, or an external portable hard drive – the choice is yours.

Follow the instructions on the screen, and eventually you'll be asked to take the Windows Vista installation disc to your old computer to run **Windows Easy Transfer** on it.

Eventually, **Windows Easy Transfer** will calculate the number of CDs or DVDs that you will require to transfer your old Accounts, Settings, and Data files, as shown in Fig. 1.11.

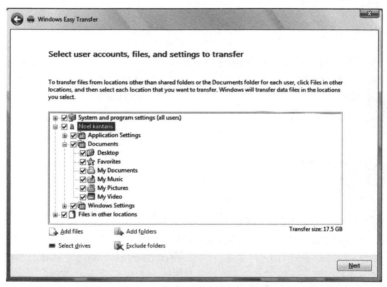

Fig. 1.11 The Welcome to Windows Easy Transfer Program.

From here you can select exactly what you want to be transferred, and you will know exactly how many CDs or DVDs you will need to accomplish the job. Perhaps now is the time to thin out some old and unwanted data.

As the choice of what you want to do is highly individual, we will leave it to you to complete the transfer. The instructions given by the program are very clear, so just follow them and you will be all right.

Once you have transferred all your required data to CD, DVD, or an external portable hard drive, then you will be told to take these to your new computer to complete the transfer.

* * *

In Chapter 2 we present an overview of Windows Vista, but without going too deep into specific topics. These will be discussed in detailed later on in the book.

* * *

2

First Impressions

The Windows Vista Starting Screen

When you switch on your PC, Windows Vista displays by default the Welcome Center in the middle of your screen as shown in Fig. 2.1 below.

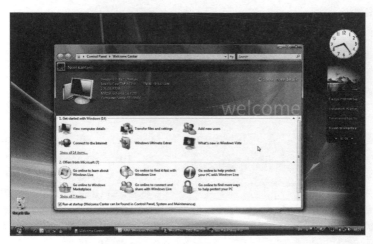

Fig. 2.1 The Windows Vista Welcome Center.

On the top third of the Welcome Center window you see details of the currently logged user with particulars of your PC's software and hardware. On the middle third of the Welcome Center window under 'Get started with Windows' you see six icons which when left-clicked give you information or start a program, such as the **View computer details** and **Add new users** icons.

Left-clicking the **Show all 14 items** link, the one just below the **Connect to the Internet** icon, displays the screen in Fig. 2.2.

Fig. 2.2 All the Windows Vista Welcome Center's Options.

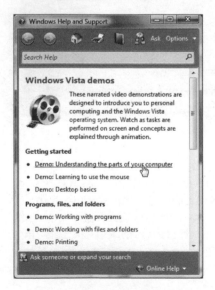

Perhaps, at this stage, you might like to explore the **Window Vista Demos** (the penultimate option) which when left-clicked display the screen in Fig. 2.3. You can even watch topics on video, which are quite interesting from an educational point of view.

Fig. 2.3 The Windows Vista Demos.

On the bottom third of the Welcome Center window under 'Offers from Microsoft' you see icons that when left-clicked attempt to connect you to the Internet (provided you have the capability), so that you can access the various offers.

If you don't want the see the Welcome Center window every time you start Windows Vista, left-click the small square at the bottom left of the window to remove the tick mark. As mentioned at the bottom of the window, the Welcome Center can be found in the **Control Panel's System and Maintenance** option – more about this later.

The Windows Sidebar

On the far right of the Windows Vista screen you will see the **Sidebar**, a new feature that allows you to connect your desktop with powerful, but easy to use 'gadgets' which are mini applications, such as the **Clock**, a photo **Slide Show**, and **News Headlines**.

Fig. 2.4 The Sidebar.

To add a gadget to the **Sidebar**, click the plus (+) sign above the **Clock** to open a Gadgets screen from which you can choose one or more to add to your **Sidebar**. You could also go online to find more gadgets. We will discuss the **Sidebar** a little more later.

The Windows Taskbar

At the bottom of the Windows Vista screen you will see the **Taskbar**.

Fig. 2.5 The Windows Taskbar.

The **Taskbar** contains the **Start** button at the extreme left which, as we will see shortly can be used to quickly start a program, followed by four **Quick Launch** buttons.

Left-clicking a **Quick Launch** button launches the corresponding application. Going from left to right these are: 'Launch Internet Explorer', 'Show desktop', 'Switch between windows', and 'Media Center'. In your case you could have a different number of **Quick Launch** buttons and appearing in a different order.

When you open a program, or a window, a button for it is placed on the **Taskbar** to the right of the **Quick Launch** buttons. In our example on the previous page we show the **Welcome Center** and the **Control Panel**.

Preview Panes and Navigation

New to Windows Vista is the ability to preview the contents of an item on the **Taskbar** without opening the item. For example, hovering with the mouse pointer over the **Welcome Center** button on the **Taskbar** opens the preview of the application as shown in Fig. 2.6 below.

Fig. 2.6 Previewing an Item on the Taskbar.

Left-clicking one of these buttons on the **Taskbar** makes the corresponding application or window active, opens it on the desktop and displays its button on the **Taskbar** in a darker shade of grey.

So, now you can always see what application windows you have open, which is the active one, and quickly switch between them.

If your PC is capable of 3D graphics, clicking the **Switch between windows** 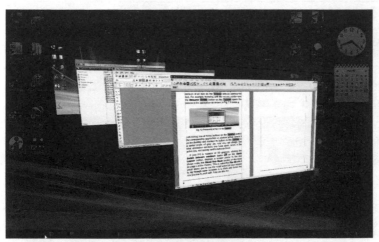 button on the **Quick Launch** toolbar, displays a screen similar to the one shown in Fig. 2.7 below. This is called the **Flip 3D** feature which allows you to use the scroll wheel on your mouse to flip through open windows in a stack and locate the one you want to work with.

Fig. 2.7 The Flip 3D Windows Vista Feature.

Try using the scroll wheel on your mouse and see the windows on the screen change position. To open a particular window, point to it and left-click.

Another useful Vista capability is the so-called **Flip** feature which allows you to flip through open windows by using the **Alt+Tab** keyboard combination (press the **Alt** key and while holding it depressed, press the **Tab** button). What you see on the screen is something similar to that shown in Fig. 2.8 on the next page.

Fig. 2.8 The Flip Windows Vista Feature.

This feature helps you to quickly identify the window you want, particularly when multiple windows of the same kind are open.

The Windows Vista Start Menu

Clicking the **Start** button displays the two-column **Start** menu as shown in Fig. 2.9. Here we show part of the Windows Vista working screen, called the 'Desktop', with the **Recycle Bin** at the bottom right of it.

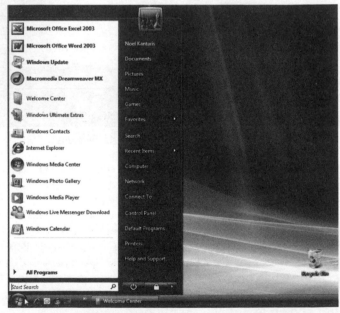

Fig. 2.9 The Windows Vista Start Menu Screen.

The left column of the **Start** menu, provides shortcuts to frequently used programs, and the nine applications used most recently (in your case these will most likely be totally different as they can be changed). On the right column there are shortcuts to **Documents**, **Pictures**, **Computer**, **Control Panel**, etc., which are normally common to all users.

If your computer is already capable of being connected to the Internet (we will show you how to do this in detail later on), you could then use the **Internet Explorer** program that comes bundled with the operating system to surf the Net, or the **Windows Mail** program to send and receive e-mail. These two programs will be discussed in some detail later on.

Windows Vista also comes with a number of features, such as **Media Center Windows Mobility Center**, **System Tools**, the **Paint** graphics program, the **Windows Photo Gallery**, and the word processor **WordPad**. Some of these will be discussed in more detail in following chapters of this book as they form the core of the tools you need to master so as to keep your computer healthy and your data safe. Of course, Windows Vista (particularly the Business and Ultimate editions) cater for many new technological capabilities, but these are beyond the scope of this book.

Program Icons and Folders

Windows Vista can manage all other programs that run on your PC, such as fully featured word processors, spreadsheets, databases, games, and many more. For example, hovering with the mouse pointer over the **All**

Programs button, shown here (also see the bottom of Fig. 2.9 for its position on the screen), displays a list of all Windows applications that are installed on your computer.

In Fig. 2.10 below, we show some of the contents of the **All Programs** available on one of our computers, as well as the contents of the Windows **Accessories**, mentioned earlier which was displayed by left-clicking the **Accessories** folder on the **All Programs** list. No more cascade menus as in Windows XP which were difficult to use particularly by Notebook users!

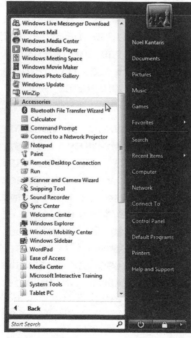

Fig. 2.10 The Programs List with the Accessories Folder Opened.

Note that in Windows Vista, programs are depicted as distinctive icons in these lists which when left-clicked start the actual program. For example, clicking the **Windows Mail** icon,

shown here, starts the e-mail program in its own window.

Folders, on the other hand, like the **Accessories** folder, can contain documents, other folders, programs or other items. To close an opened folder on this list, left-click it once more.

The Start Search Box

The **Start Search** box is found above the Windows **Start** button (see Fig. 2.10) and is shown in Fig. 2.11 below.

Fig. 2.11 The Start Search Box.

The **Start Search** facility is the quickest way of finding a document, e-mail, or picture, by typing a keyword in the box. Type the word *Microsoft* and see what is listed. Left-clicking a program·on this list, starts the actual program.

The search facility is of paramount importance to Windows Vista. In fact, you will find a **Search** box on every folder that you open. We will discuss folders and files in some detail in Chapter 4.

Fig. 2.12 The Searches folder.

New to Windows Vista is another kind of folder, as shown in Fig. 2.12, called **Virtual Folder** which is simply a saved search that is instantly run when you open the folder. In our case the **Searches** folder contains a number of other virtual folders. Later on, when you click on such a virtual folder, Windows Vista runs the search and provides immediate results.

Using the Help System

To obtain help in Windows Vista, click the **Start** button, then click the **Help and Support** menu option which opens the main Help window, shown in Fig. 2.13.

The **What's new** option gives you a good idea of all the topics that are new to Windows Vista, while the **Windows Basics** option provides you with specific information about your computer, the Windows environment, and other topics. Left-clicking this option displays an extraordinary number of hypertext links to various topics. Clicking such a hypertext link, can open up a further list of hypertext links until you home onto the specific subject you are searching for.

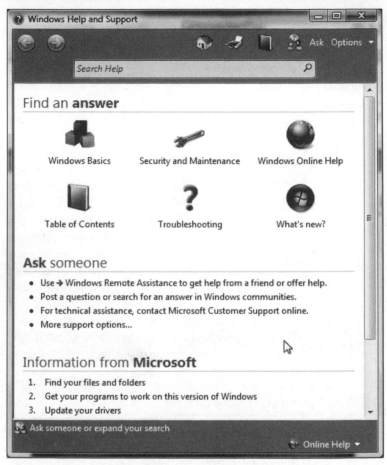

Fig. 2.13 The Windows Vista Help and Support Center.

The **Search Help** facility gives you access to a very powerful individual word search of the **Help** system, as shown in Fig. 2.14 on the next page. For example, if you wanted to know something about e-mail, type the word *e-mail* in the **Search Help** box and click the 🔎 button to have Windows display almost everything there is to know about e-mail.

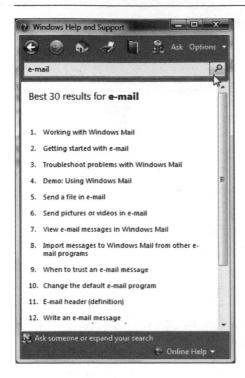

If you can't find what you are looking for off-line, you can always click the **Windows Online Help** button on the **Help and Support** screen.

It might be worth your while spending some time here investigating the various options available to you, particularly if you are new to Windows.

Fig. 2.14 Using the Help Search Facility.

User Accounts

At the top of the **Start** menu the name of the current user is displayed with a picture against it. Left-clicking this picture opens the User Accounts screen shown in Fig. 2.15. From here you can create a user password, choose a different picture for the current user, change your account name, etc.

Note the **Search** box at the top right of the screen in Fig. 2.15 shown on the next page. It is to be found everywhere!

Fig. 2.15 The User Accounts Dialogue Box.

Changing the Start Menu

As we mentioned earlier, Windows Vista has the ability to adapt the first of its two-column menus to the way you use your PC. It keeps track of what features and programs you use the most and adds them to the list at the bottom of the left column. For example, if you use **WordPad** a couple of times by selecting it from the **Accessories** sub-menu, next time you click the **Start** button you will see this application pinned to the bottom half of the first column of the **Start** menu.

This saves time as you don't have to scroll through

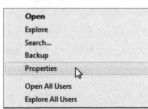

Fig. 2.16 The Context Sensitive Start Button Menu.

menu lists to find the application you want to use. However, should you want to deactivate this feature, right-click the **Start** button and select **Properties** from the context sensitive menu (more about this shortly), as shown in Fig. 2.16.

This opens the Taskbar and Start Menu Properties screen, shown in Fig. 2.17, and clicking the **Store and display a list of recently opened files** box to uncheck it, removes the feature.

Fig. 2.17 The Taskbar and Start Menu Properties Screen.

To remove an application from the first column of the **Start** menu, right-click it with your mouse and select **Remove from this list**, as shown in Fig. 2.18. This removes the name of the application from the list, not the application itself from your hard disc.

You also have a menu option to **Pin to Start Menu** any selected program.

Fig. 2.18 Simultaneous Display of Running Applications.

You can also use this facility to pin your favourite programs to the top half of the left column of the **Start** menu, even if these are to be found in the **All Programs** menu or its sub-menus, thus customising the way you run your computer. Try pinning **WordPad** to the **Start** menu – you will find having **WordPad** accessible rather useful later.

Some programs when installed on your PC place a shortcut icon on your desktop. Right-clicking such an icon displays the same options as above so you can pin it to either the **Start** menu or the **Quick Launch** menu.

Moving Start Menu Shortcuts

Once you have pinned your chosen programs to the **Start** menu, you could rename them, if you so wished, using the right-click menu, or you could move their position on the list to suit your preferences.

To move an item on the **Start** menu, point to it to highlight it, then press the left mouse button and while keeping it pressed, drag the mouse pointer to the desired position on the list. Letting go of the mouse button, fixes the item in the chosen position. Fig. 2.19 shows Microsoft Word being moved to just below Microsoft Excel.

Fig. 2.19 Moving an Application on the **Start** Menu List.

Context Sensitive Menus

To see another context sensitive menu (also known as a shortcut or right-click menu) containing the most common commands applicable to, say, the desktop, point with

your mouse to an empty part of it and right-click. This displays the menu shown in Fig. 2.20. From this menu you can select how to **Sort** icons on your desktop, **Paste** a shortcut icon on it, or create a **New** folder for your favourite program. Items on the pull-down sub-menu which are marked with an arrow ▶ to their right, as shown here, open up additional options when selected

Fig. 2.20 The Desktop Right-click Menu.

Right-clicking the **Recycle Bin** icon on the desktop, reveals the options in Fig. 2.21. In this case we have the option to **Open** the **Recycle Bin** which has the same effect as double-clicking its icon with the left mouse button, **Explore** its contents, **Empty** it of its contents, or display its **Properties**.

Fig. 2.21 The Recycle Bin Right-click Menu.

If you were to right-click a program icon on the **All Programs** menu, such as that of a word processor, if one was installed on your computer, you would find that different options to those of the **Recycle Bin** are being offered. Unlike Windows XP, in Windows Vista you have the option to delete or rename the **Recycle Bin**, but we do not recommend you do so.

Changing a User's Picture

To change the picture that represents you as a user, left-click the **Start** button to display its menu. Next, place the mouse pointer on the picture at the top right of the **Start** menu (your picture could be different to the one shown here), and when it changes to a pointing hand, as shown to the right, left-click it  to open the User Accounts window, and click the **Change your picture** link to open the screen shown in Fig. 2.22.

Fig. 2.22 The User Accounts Pictures.

You can select a different picture to represent you by left-clicking one from the displayed list and clicking the **Change Picture** button at the bottom of the screen.

Exiting Windows Vista

To exit Windows, click the **Start** button and hover with the mouse pointer over the right arrow button ■ (next to the **Lock this Computer** button 🔒). This opens the additional options as shown in Fig. 2.23.

Fig. 2.23 The Lower Part of the Start Menu.

From here you can select to **Switch User**, **Log Off** the current user and leave the computer running so another user can take over by logging on (make sure you save all your work), **Lock** the Computer (a password, if you set one, will be required to log in again), **Restart** the computer (used if you want to clear the memory settings and restart Windows), put your computer in a **Sleep** mode (low power mode so that you can get back to your work quickly), **Hibernate** the computer (all your work is saved to disc and when you restart everything is as you left it), or **Shut Down** the computer which requires a fresh start of Windows.

The **Lock this Computer** button 🔒 does exactly what it says – it locks your PC and you will need a password (if you set one) to access it, while the **Power** button ⏻ puts your PC on a low power state keeping all programs in memory so you can access your work quickly.

Note: With Windows Vista, just as with Windows XP, you can just switch off your computer – the **Shut Down** procedure will then be carried out automatically.

An Exit Strategy for Notebook Users

If you have a notebook, you might find, even at the very early stages of ownership, that you would like to change what happens when you press the notebook's power button from the default 'Sleep' to, say, Hibernate. After all, closing the notebook's lid already puts it to sleep.

When Hibernating, the PC writes all your current work to disc, so that they can be reloaded when you start, without having to go through a reboot of the system (which takes longer). You use Hibernation for much longer periods (overnight) away from your PC.

To change the default power setting, right-click the **Battery Indicator** button in the **System Tray** to display the context sensitive menu shown in Fig. 2.24 below.

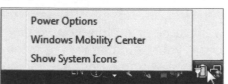

Left-clicking the **Power Options** opens the dialogue box shown in Fig. 2.25.

Fig. 2.24 The context Sensitive Menu of the Battery Indicator.

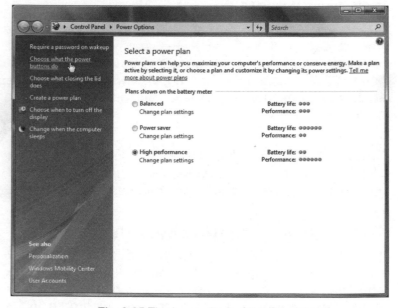

Fig. 2.25 The Lower Part of the Start Menu.

As you can see from the above Power Options screen, you can control just about everything relating to the power of your notebook. However, here we will only deal with the second option (pointed to above). Clicking this option opens a further screen, as shown in Fig. 2.26 on the next page.

Fig. 2.26 The Lower Part of the Start Menu.

Use the down arrows to the right of the selection boxes to reveal options for what happens when you press the power button of your notebook. Above we show our choice. The other power options will be discussed in some detail later on, so we will leave this topic for now.

* * *

In the next chapter we discuss the Windows environment with its Explorer type windows, their navigation buttons, and menu bar options, so that you can find your way around your documents and programs. We then show you how to manipulate windows on the desktop by sizing, moving, minimising, maximising and displaying them in different ways on the screen.

* * *

3

The Vista Environment

Windows Vista drops the **My** from the names of its various personal folders, so now instead of 'My Documents', or 'My Pictures' (which was the name convention in Windows XP), the folders are named simply **Documents**, **Pictures**, **Music**, etc., but it is understood that they belong to the currently logged user.

To see your folders, click the **Start** ⊙ button and then click your name (or the name you use to log into your PC) at the top of the displayed menu (see Fig. 2.7 on page 19). This opens a window similar to the one in Fig. 3.1.

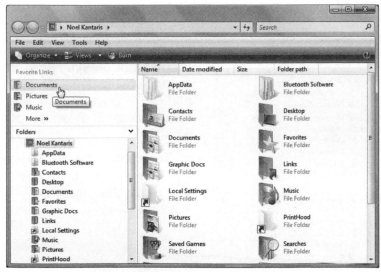

Fig. 3.1 The Display of Personal Folders.

The Vista Window

At the left pane of the Explorer-type window, called the **Navigation** pane, your **Favorite Links** are listed (their spelling, not ours), while at the right pane you will find your **Folders** list. Placing the mouse pointer on a **Navigation** link until it changes to a pointing hand (as shown in Fig. 3.1) and left-clicking it, displays the contents of the linked folder. Alternatively, left-clicking a folder in the **Folders List** pane does the same thing.

You can also display the folders tree associated with this window by clicking the arrow to the right of the

Folders entry, as shown here, to be found at the bottom of the **Navigation** pane. This displays a screen similar to that in Fig. 3.2.

The **Folders** tree provides instant navigation starting from your Desktop. It could not be simpler – no more hunting deep through endless 'Documents and Settings' to find what you want!

To close the **Folders** tree, left-click the down arrow to the right of the **Folders** pane.

Fig. 3.2 The Folders Tree.

Parts of a Window

A typical Vista window is subdivided into several areas, such as the **Address Bar**, **Search Bar**, **Folders Tree**, and also includes navigation buttons, and command buttons. These have the following functions:

Area	*Function*	
Minimise button	Clicking the **Minimise** button (at the top right of the window) stores an application as an icon on the **Taskbar**. Clicking on such an icon will restore the window.	
Maximise button	Clicking the **Maximise** button (also at the top right of the window) fills the screen with the active window. When that happens, the **Maximise** button changes to a **Restore Down** button which can be used to restore the window to its former size.	
Close button	The extreme top right button that you click to close a window.	
Navigation buttons	The **Go Back** (left) button takes you to the previous display, while the **Go Forward** (right) button takes you to the next display.	

Quick search box	The box in which you type your search criteria. As you start typing the first few letters, the displayed files filter down to just the matching terms. This makes finding your documents, programs, and media files much easier.
Address bar	Shows the location of the current folder, or the URL (Uniform Resource Locator) of the new Web page to go to next.
Menu bar	The bar which only displays if you press the **Alt** key. It allows you to choose from several menu options. Clicking on a menu item displays the pull-down menu associated with that item.
Toolbar	A bar of icons that you click to carry out some common actions. The icons displayed on the toolbar depend on the specific application.
Scroll bars/buttons	The bars/buttons at the extreme right and bottom of each window (or pane within a window) that contain a scroll box/button. Clicking on these allows you to see parts of a document that might not be visible in that size window.

There are other areas or panes that can be made to display in a document or application window. For example you can activate a **Details Pane**, or a **Preview Pane**. These are discussed in some detail in the next section.

Below we show the tops of two Explorer-type window screens, one that heads the **Pictures** folder and the other that heads the **Computer** folder which is opened by clicking on the **Start** button and then clicking its entry on the right column of the Windows **Start** menu. Note that we use the word 'Windows' to refer to the whole environment, while the word 'windows' refers to document or application windows. To see the **Menu bar** press the **Alt** key (more about this later).

Fig. 3.3 The Top of the Pictures Screen.

Fig. 3.4 The Top of the Computer Window.

Both these windows look remarkably the same. The only part that has changed is the content of the toolbar, which in Windows Vista changes automatically to reflect the type of work you might want to do with the contents of the specific folder or application.

Also note that the window of Fig. 3.4 was placed on top of the **Clock** of the Windows **Sidebar** to show that the windows on our desktop are translucent. This is the Aero experience of Vista, but you will only see it if your graphics card is capable of it. The borders of each window blur objects lying under them, leaving the window you are working on in focus. However, if you find this feature annoying, you can switch it off. This might be welcomed by notebook users, as this overrated feature uses extra battery power!

To turn off the Aero feature, left-click the **Start** button and click the **Control Panel** option on the right column of the displayed menu list (more about the **Control Panel** later). This opens the screen in Fig. 3.5.

Fig. 3.5 The Control Panel Screen.

Next, click the **Customize colors** link to open the screen in Fig. 3.6. Finally, click the **Enable transparency** box to remove the check mark.

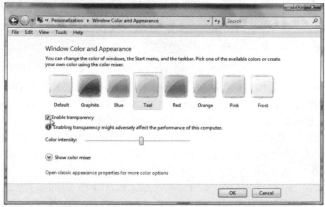

Fig. 3.6 The Window Color and Appearance Screen.

Additional Window Panes

We have already seen how you can activate the **Navigation** pane in a Windows Vista screen. You can further activate two additional panes by clicking the **Organize** toolbar button, selecting **Layout** from the drop-down menu, and clicking the following options in turn:

Option	*Function*
Details pane	To display information on an item without opening it.
Preview pane	To preview selected items.
Navigation pane	To display the navigation tree.

The screen in Fig. 3.7 displays all these panes open with the **Preview** pane on the right of the screen, and the **Details** pane at the bottom of the screen.

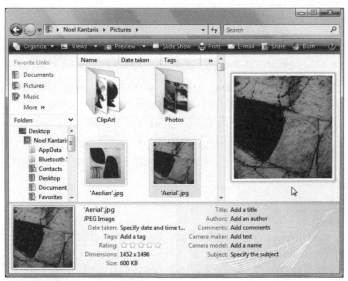

Fig. 3.7 The Four Panes Surrounding the Display Area.

You can also use the **Organize**, **Layout** option to activate the Menu Bar (more about this shortly).

The Mouse Pointers

Windows has many different mouse pointers, with the most common illustrated below, which it uses for its various functions. When a program is initially started up probably the first you will see is the rotating circle, which eventually turns into an upward pointing hollow arrow. Some of the shapes, as shown below, depend on the type of work you are doing at the time.

The rotating circle which displays when you are waiting while performing a function.

The arrow which appears when the pointer is placed over menus, scroll bars, and buttons.

The I-beam which appears in normal text areas of the screen.

The large 4-headed arrow which appears after choosing the Control, Move/Size command(s) for moving or sizing windows.

The double arrows which appear when over the border of a window, used to drag the side and alter the size of the window.

The Help hand which appears in the help windows, and is used to access 'hypertext' type links.

Windows applications, such as word processors, spreadsheets and databases, can have additional mouse pointers which facilitate the execution of selected commands, such as highlighting text or defining areas.

The Menu Bar Options

A window's **Menu Bar** can be activated using the **Organize**, **Layout**, **Menu Bar** option (or you can display it temporarily by pressing the **Alt** key). Each displayed **Menu Bar** command has associated with it a pull-down sub-menu. To activate a menu option, point to it with the mouse to highlight it and click the left mouse button. As the mouse pointer is moved onto each of the sub-menu options it highlights it. To activate a sub-menu option, highlight it and click the left mouse button.

The sub-menu of the **Edit** option of the **Pictures** folder window, is shown in Fig. 3.8. Here we have deactivated the **Preview** and **Details** panes by selecting them once more from the **Organize**, **Layout** toolbar.

Fig. 3.8 Menu Bar Options.

Note the **Select All** option; very useful for easily selecting all the items in a folder (more about item selection later).

The options displayed on the **Menu Bar** of different Windows applications might differ from the ones shown in Fig. 3.7. Nevertheless, all these options are self-explanatory and we will leave to you to explore. Do note, however, that having activated a menu, you can close it without taking any further action by simply left-clicking the mouse pointer somewhere else on the screen, or by simply pressing the **Esc** key.

Dialogue Boxes

Three periods after a sub-menu option or command, indicate that a dialogue box will open when the option or command is selected. A dialogue box is used for the insertion of additional information, such as a filename.

To see a dialogue box, click the **Start** button and select the **Computer** menu option. Next, press the **Alt** key to display the **Menu bar**, click **Tools** and on the drop-down sub-menu select **Folder Options**. This opens the Folder Options dialogue box with its General tab selected. In Fig. 3.9 on the next page we show this dialogue box with its View tab selected so that you can see two different types of option lists.

When a dialogue box opens, the **Tab** key can be used to move the dotted rectangle (known as the focus) from one field to another. Alternatively you can use the mouse to left-click directly the desired field.

Some dialogue boxes contain List boxes which show a column of available choices. If there are more choices than can be seen in the area provided, use the scroll bars to reveal them.

Such dialogue boxes may contain Check boxes, as shown to the left, which offer a list of features you can switch on or off. Selected options show a tick in the box against the option name.

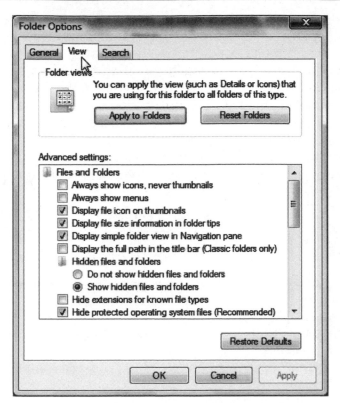

Fig. 3.9 The Folder Options Dialogue Box.

Another type of option available in this dialogue box is the Option button (sometimes called Radio button) with a list of mutually exclusive items. The default choice is marked with a black dot against its name, while unavailable options are dimmed.

Another type of List box may display a column of document files. To select a single file from such a List box, either double-click the file, or use the arrow keys to highlight the file and press **Enter**. Again, if there are more files than can be seen in the area provided, use the scroll bars to reveal them.

Other dialogue boxes may contain groups of options within a field. In such cases, you can use the arrow keys to move from one option to another. Having selected an option or typed in information in a text box, you must press a command button, such as the **OK**, **Cancel** or **Apply** button (unavailable options or command buttons are dimmed), or choose from additional options. To select the **OK** button with the mouse, simply point and left-click, while with the keyboard, you must first press the **Tab** key until the focus moves to the required button, and then press the **Enter** key.

To cancel a dialogue box, either press the **Cancel** button, or the **Esc** key enough times to close the dialogue box and then the menu system.

Note: At this stage it might be a good time to change the default settings under the **View** tab of Fig. 2.8 by removing the check mark (click on the box to toggle it off) beside the **Hide extensions for known file types** option. Doing so could alert you to rogue and potentially lethal e-mail attachments.

The Taskbar and Start Menu Properties

As described in the previous chapter, at the bottom of the Desktop screen is the **Taskbar** to the right of the **Start** button which, as we have seen, can be used to quickly start a program (from the **Quick Launch** toolbar), or switch between running programs whose minimised icon is shown on the **Taskbar**.

To display the properties of the **Taskbar**, right-click an empty part of the **Taskbar**, and select **Properties** from the displayed menu, as shown in Fig. 3.10 on the next page.

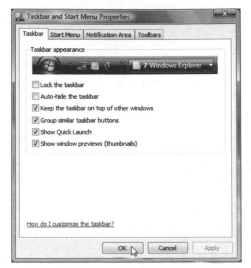

Fig. 3.10 The Taskbar and Start Menu
Properties Tabbed Screen.

From the **Taskbar** tabbed screen, you can configure your **Taskbar** by locking it, auto-hiding it, or keeping it on top of other windows. From here you can also choose to show the **Quick Launch** toolbar or not.

You might have noticed by now that as more buttons are placed on the **Taskbar** their size shrinks slightly, but up to a point. After that, common entries are grouped together with a number indicating the number of open windows, provided the appropriate box in Fig. 3.10 is ticked. To see details relating to a grouped button, move the mouse pointer on it on the **Taskbar** to display Fig. 3.11a and click it to open a list of components, as shown in Fig. 3.11b.

(a)   (b)

Fig. 3.11 Grouped Taskbar Entries.

To close a group of running programs, right-click their button on the **Taskbar** and select **Close Group** from the displayed menu.

Do investigate the other tab screens of the **Taskbar and Start Menu Properties** dialogue box (Fig. 3.10), to see how you can configure your PC to your liking. For example, if you want to preserve your privacy, click the Start Menu tab, and in the displayed screen remove the check marks from the two boxes under **Privacy**. This stops the listing of recently opened files and programs.

Manipulating Windows

To use any Windows program effectively, you will need to be able to manipulate a series of windows, to select which one is to be active, to move them, or change their size, so that you can see all the relevant parts of each one. What follows is a short discussion on how to achieve this.

Changing the Active Window

To select the active window amongst those displayed on the screen (these will only be displayed on the screen simultaneously if their **Restore Down** 🔳 button has been left-clicked), point to it and click the left mouse button, or, if the one you want to activate is not visible, click its icon on the **Taskbar**.

Sizing a Window

You can change the size of a window with the mouse by

first moving the window so that the side you want to change is visible, then moving the mouse pointer to the edge of the window or corner so that it changes to a two-headed arrow, then dragging the two-headed arrow in the direction you want that side or corner to move.

Moving Windows and Dialogue Boxes

To move a window (or a dialogue box) with the mouse, point to its title bar (see Fig. 3.12), and drag it until it is where you want it to be on the screen, then release the mouse button. This can only be achieved if the window does not occupy the full screen.

Fig. 3.12 Moving a Window with the Mouse.

Minimising and Maximising Windows

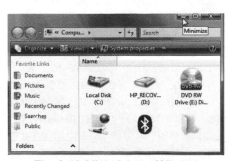

Fig. 3.13 Minimising a Window.

To minimise a window into a **Taskbar** icon (to temporarily free up desktop space) left-click the **Minimize** button in the upper-right corner of the window, also shown in Fig. 3.13.

To maximise a window so that it fills the entire screen, left-click the **Maximize**  button in the upper right corner of the window.

An application which has been minimised or maximised can be returned to its original size and position on the screen by either clicking on its **Taskbar** icon to expand it to a window, or clicking on the **Restore Down** button of the maximised window, to reduce it to its former size.

Closing a Window

A document window can be closed at any time to save screen space and memory. To do this, left-click the Close button. If you try to close a window of an application document, such as that of a word processor, in which you have made changes since the last time you saved it, you will get a warning in the form of a dialogue box asking confirmation prior to closing it. This safeguards against loss of information.

Windows Display Arrangement

In Windows and most Windows application programs, you can display multiple windows in both tiled (side by side) and cascaded (overlapping) forms – the choice being a matter of balance between personal preference and the type of work you are doing at the time. If you want to organise these automatically, right-click on an empty part of the Taskbar which opens the menu shown in Fig. 3.14.

Fig. 3.14 The Taskbar Shortcut Menu.

In Fig. 3.15 we show the **Cascade Windows** option, while in Fig. 3.16, we show the **Side by Side Windows** option.

Fig. 3.15 Windows Displayed in Cascade Form.

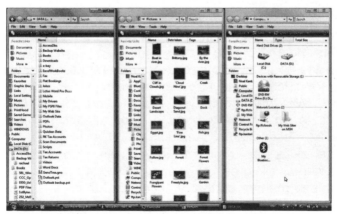

Fig. 3.16 Windows Displayed in Side by Side Form.

As we have discussed earlier, the size of these windows can be changed, hence you might have to alter their size to display exactly what is displayed in Fig. 3.15 and Fig. 3.16. The contents, of course, will not be the same.

You might like to practise what we have described above by opening the two utilities, **Computer** and **Control Panel** from the **Start** menu, then display their windows in stacked form by right-clicking an empty area of the **Taskbar** and selecting **Show Windows Stacked** from the displayed shortcut menu, then display the two windows in the **Side by Side** form (this is Microsoft's terminology, not ours), to see which version you prefer.

Finally, and while the two utilities mentioned above are opened, start the **Printers** utility and remind yourself how these three windows look in **Flip** and **Flip 3D** (see page 19). It is worth while comparing all four methods of displaying opened windows. We rather like the **Flip 3D** feature, particularly when combined with the scroll wheel of the mouse.

* * *

In the next chapter we discuss how to navigate between folders, how to create a new folder, and how to name it and rename it, how to search your computer for specific files (or folders) and copy or move them into the new folder. We then show you how to create application shortcuts, followed by how to send files or folders to specific destinations, including a CD or DVD writer. These skills are required if you want to keep your documents, pictures, and music files in some sort of organised manner so that you can find them later quickly and easily. Finally, we discuss the **Recycle Bin** in which deleted files and folders are kept until you decide whether you want them after all or delete them for good.

* * *

4

Using Folders & Files in Vista

In this chapter we discuss the skills you will need to keep your data organised so that you can easily find your documents, pictures or music files at a later stage. Windows provides you with the means to keep such files in folders which you can create for the purpose, copy files into them, or even delete unwanted files from them. Folders, which can also contain other folders, are kept on your hard disc which is not dissimilar to the idea of a filing cabinet, if one is to use an analogy.

It is possible, of course, that you might have more than one fixed hard disc (as we do – see Fig. 3.12), or that you might have one or more removable hard discs attached to your system. Whether you have such additional *filing cabinets* or not, is not important as the skills required to keep one organised can also be applied to the others.

Windows provides you, by default, with five folders for each user, called **Documents**, **Pictures**, **Music**, **Games**, and **Favorites**, all of which can be accessed from the **Start** menu. In each of these folders there might be other folders.

In what follows, we will carry on with this structured tradition, so that folders we create for word processed data, spreadsheet workbooks, etc., are also contained within the **Documents** folder. In this way, when you left-click **Documents** on the **Start** menu, all the other folders will be available to you.

The Address Bar

To discuss how the **Address Bar** in Windows Vista is

used to navigate through your folders, left-click the **Start** button and click the **Pictures** option near the top of the right column of the displayed menu, as shown in Fig. 4.1.

Note that here we have selected the **Pictures** menu option directly rather than selecting a user first, then his or her **Pictures**. The contents of what displays is the same, but what appears on the **Address Bar** is different, as shown by comparing Fig. 4.2 below with Fig. 3.8 (see page 43).

Fig. 4.1 Selecting the Pictures Folder from the Start Menu.

Fig. 4.2 The Displayed Pictures Folder for our PC.

The reason for this difference in the contents of the **Address Bar**, is that Windows Vista dispenses with the old hierarchical drive:\folder\sub-folder\file approach to navigation found in Windows XP and replaces it with what is dubbed as the "breadcrumb" approached. This was partly necessary to accommodate the new **Virtual** folders in which the results of searches are kept.

Below, we show the **Address Bar** of Fig. 4.2 enlarged and after clicking on the **Photos** sub-folder.

Fig. 4.3 A Folder's Address Bar.

You might wonder why we have a sub-folder called **Photos** within the **Pictures** folder. We personally store selected pictures in the **Pictures** folder and use these as our screen saver (more about this in the next chapter), while in the **Photos** folder we keep all our personal photographs within additional, and dated, sub-folders.

Returning to the **Address Bar**, if you hover with the mouse pointer on an entry, the right arrow between the two entries in the **Address Bar**, or the double chevron to the left of the **Pictures** entry, you will see that they glow blue, indicating that they are buttons.

Fig. 4.4 A Folder's Address Bar.

Clicking the right arrow button between the two **Address Bar** entries, changes it to a down-arrow, and displays a drop-down menu, as shown in Fig. 4.4, with the currently selected **Photos** sub-folder shown emboldened. From here you can select a different **Pictures** sub-folder.

Clicking the double chevron button to the left of the **Pictures** entry, pointed to in Fig. 4.5, displays a drop-down menu which you can use to jump to key locations. The emboldened entry on the menu indicates the parent directory of the currently displayed first entry in the **Address Bar**.

Fig. 4.5 A Folder's Address Bar.

Clicking the down-arrow to the left of the **Address Bar**, displays a list of recently visited pages, while clicking the down-arrow to the far right of the **Address Bar** (and to the left of the **Refresh** 🔄 button), displays a list of previously visited locations, as shown in the composite in Fig. 4.6 (see page 48 if you want to clear such a list).

Fig. 4.6 A Folder's Address Bar.

Finally, you can use the two arrow ◐◑buttons to navigate to a previously location with the left button, and having done so, you can return to the current location with the right button.

It is also worth noting that to the far right of the **Address Bar**, there is a **Search** box, so you can easily find folders and their content (more about this shortly).

Creating a New Folder

In what follows we will create a new folder, name it, and rename it. To create a new folder within, say **Pictures**, left-click the **Start** button to display its menu, then click **Pictures** at the top of the right column of the menu to display Fig. 4.7 below (in your case the contents of this will be different).

If one of the pictures in the folder is highlighted, it displays enlarged in the **Preview** pane of the window, as shown on the right pane in Fig. 4.7 below.

Next, click the **Organize** toolbar icon, then point and click the **New Folder** entry, as shown in **Folder's** tree in Fig. 4.7.

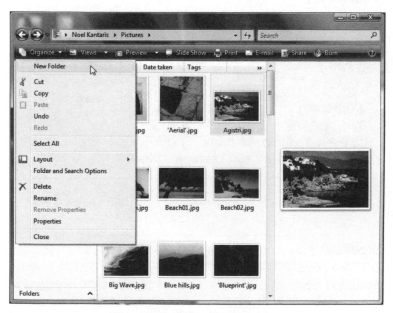

Fig. 4.7 Creating a New Folder.

To Name a newly created folder, which Windows calls **New Folder** and places it at the end of the list of existing items, just type a new name, say, **Photos**, which replaces the default highlighted name given to it by Windows.

You can rename a folder or a file using two different methods, as follows:

Method 1

Click the folder or file you want to rename to select it, then clicking it once more will display the insertion pointer within its name. Type a different name to replace the existing one.

Method 2

Click the folder or file you want to rename to select it (in this example we chose a folder), then click the **Organize** toolbar icon and select **Rename** from the drop-down menu which causes the insertion pointer to be displayed within its name. Type a different name to replace the existing one.

Fig. 4.8 The Organize Sub-menu.

Searching for Files and Folders

Windows Vista has a new **Search** facility which appears on the right column of the **Start** menu, and in every Explorer type window. To investigate this facility, left-click the **Start** menu and select the **Search** option. This opens the Search window shown in Fig. 4.9 on the next page.

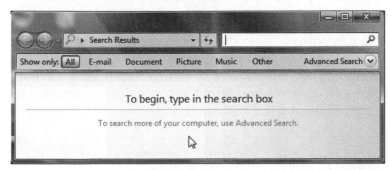

Fig. 4.9 The Search Window.

As you type letters in the **Search** box, Windows starts returning results and narrows them down as you type more letters. Below, we show the results of the search after typing the three letters 'aeo' in the **Search** bar.

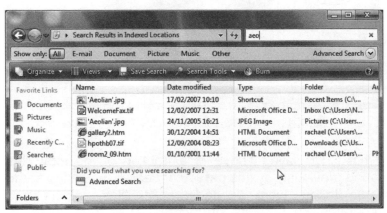

Fig. 4.10 The Search Results.

Note that in this case, the search results includes **All** files, folders, and programs, as shown in Fig. 4.10, and that the three letters we typed in the **Search** box, appear in the results, but not in any specific order.

Narrowing Search Results

You can narrow down the search criteria, by selecting to only display results from **E-mail** messages, **Document** folder and its sub-folders, **Picture** folder and its sub-folders, etc., which reduces the results of the search, as shown in Fig. 4.11.

Fig. 4.11 Search Results within the Picture Folder.

What is displayed above is a fraction of the total files found previously by this particular search, when the same three letters were applied to **All** files, folders and programs. Your results, of course, will be totally different from ours.

The **Search** utility includes a **Search Tools** button which, when clicked, displays a drop-down sub-menu with three options. Left-clicking **Search options** displays the 3-tabbed dialogue box shown in Fig. 4.12 on the next page.

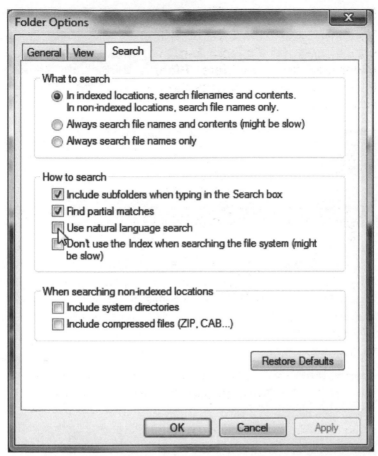

Fig. 4.12 The Search Screen of the Folder Options Dialogue Box.

Checking the **Use natural language search** box, allows you to search for, say, **E-mail** messages using words like 'messages sent last week'. The result of our search is shown in Fig. 4.13 on the next page, with the highlighted message displaying in the **Preview** pane.

Making the **Search** window larger, reveals more details, such as the times the messages were sent, their size, etc.

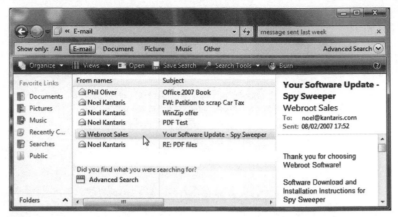

Fig. 4.13 The Search Results Applied to E-mail Messages.

With Windows Vista you can use the **Save Search** button on the toolbar to save the search criteria you have used together with the search results in a **Virtual** folder. Subsequently, every time you click such a **Virtual** folder Windows runs the search and provides new results.

Another button on the Windows **Search** toolbar is the **Views** button with its associated sub-menu. You can choose to display items in a variety of ways as shown in Fig. 4.14. Do try to find out which of these you prefer.

Fig. 4.14 The View Sub-menu.

Selecting Files and Folders

What we demonstrate below with files could also be done with folders, or a mixture of files and folders within any folder. Here we use the files in the **Sample Pictures** sub-folder of the **Pictures** folder which comes with Vista.

To select several objects, or icons, you have three options:

- If they form a contiguous list, as shown in Fig. 4.15 below, left-click the first in the list, then with the **Shift** key depressed, click the last in the list.

Fig. 4.15 Selecting Items in a Folder.

- To select random objects hold the **Ctrl** key down and left-click them, one by one.

- To select all the items in a window first press the **Alt** key to display the **Menu** bar, then use the **Edit**, **Select All** menu command.

To cancel a selection, click in an empty area of the window.

Copying or Moving Files and Folders

When you *copy* a file or folder to somewhere else, the original version of the folder or file is not altered or removed, but when you *move* a folder or file to a new location, the original is actually deleted.

To copy selected items into a target folder, right-click the selected items and choose the **Copy** option from the shortcut menu as shown in Fig. 4.16 below.

Fig. 4.16 Copying Selected Files to the Clipboard.

The selected files are then copied to the Windows **Clipboard** which is a temporary storage area of memory where text and graphics are stored with the Windows **Cut** and **Copy** actions.

All you need to do now is navigate to the **Photos** folder, double-click it to open it, create a new folder (call it **Sample Pictures**), double-click it to open it, then right-click it and select the **Paste** option from the displayed shortcut menu.

Creating Shortcuts

With Windows you can put a shortcut to any program or document on your desktop or in any folder. Shortcuts are quick ways to get to the items you use often; they save you having to dig into menus to access them.

One program that you might want to access quickly, to say write a quick letter, is **WordPad**, so we will step you through the process of finding and placing a shortcut to it on the desktop.

As **WordPad** is in the **Accessories** folder, to locate it use the **Start**, **All Programs**, **Accessories** menu option. Next, highlight **WordPad**, right-click it, and select **Send To**, **Desktop (create shortcut)** option, as shown in Fig. 4.19.

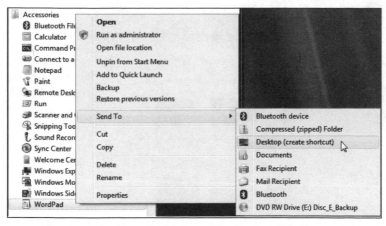

Fig. 4.19 Placing a Shortcut to WordPad on the Desktop.

Double-clicking such a shortcut icon on the desktop will be easier and quicker than digging deep into the menus to open the program.

Deleting Files or Folders

Before we delete any folders and their contents, let us create a duplicate of one so we don't delete anything valuable. To do this, first open the **Sample Pictures** folder (found in the **Pictures** folder), select all items and copy them on the **Clipboard** (refer to Fig, 4.16 for the method). Next, left-click the **Pictures** entry under the **Favorite Links** to open its folder, right-click on an empty part of it and select **Paste** from the drop-down menu, as shown in Fig. 4.20 below.

Fig. 4.20 Pasting a Selection of Items into a Folder.

Note that now the items in the **Sample Pictures** are to be found in both the **Pictures** folder and in their original folder which is a bit of duplication, but now we can show you how to delete unwanted items.

To delete or remove items (files or folders), first highlight them, and then either select the **Organize**, **Delete** ✕ option, right-click them and selected **Delete**, or press the **Del** key on the keyboard. All of these methods open the confirmation box shown in Fig. 4.21 which gives you the chance to abort the operation by selecting **No**.

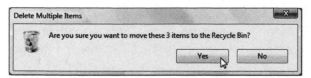

Fig. 4.21 The Delete Files Warning Dialogue Box.

To delete a folder, follow the same procedure as for files. Deleting a single folder displays the dialogue box shown in Fig 4.22.

A similar elaborate dialogue box also displays when

you try to delete a single file. To carry on with the deletion in either case, select **Yes**.

Fig. 4.22 The Delete Folder Warning Box.

Another way of deleting selected items is to right-click them and choose the **Delete** option from the drop-down menu. Either method removes such items from your hard disc and places them in the **Recycle Bin**.

Now is the time to delete any duplicate image files that you don't want to keep. Do carry out this suggestion as we need to demonstrate what happens to deleted items next.

The Recycle Bin

As you can see from the message boxes on the previous page, by default all files or folders deleted from a hard disc, are actually placed in a holding folder named the **Recycle Bin**.

If you open the **Recycle Bin**, by double-clicking its desktop icon, shown here, you will see that it is just a special folder. It lists all the files, folders, icons and shortcuts that have been deleted from fixed drives since it was last emptied, as shown in Fig. 4.23. To see the display as it appears below, use the **Views**, **Medium Icons** menu option.

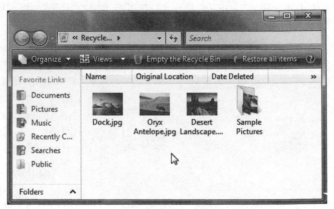

Fig. 4.23 The Recycle Bin Folder Showing Deleted Items.

Windows keeps a record of the original locations of the deleted items, so that it can restore them if necessary. To restore or delete all the items in the **Recycle Bin**, click the **Restore all items** or **Empty the Recycle Bin** option.

To restore specific files or folders from the **Recycle Bin**, first select them, which changes the toolbar options, then use the appropriate toolbar button. To delete an item, select it and press the **Delete** keyboard key.

Copying Files or Folders to a CD

To copy files or folders to a CD, you will need a recordable compact disc (CD-R) or a rewritable compact disc (CD-RW) and a CD recorder. To start the process, insert a blank recordable or rewritable CD in the CD recorder, then click the **Computer** entry in the **Start** menu and locate and select the files or folder you want to copy to the CD. Make sure that the selected files or folder contents do not exceed the CD's capacity (650 MB for a standard CD). We used the **Photos** folder for this exercise and burned it on a rewritable DVD (4.7 GB capacity).

Next, click the **Burn** button on the toolbar menu option, as shown in Fig. 4.24.

Fig. 4.24 Copying Selected Files to a CD.

The burning process is then started and a Copying notification box is displayed, as shown in Fig. 4.25 on the next page. This method is excellent for making backups of your important data (see Chapter 14, page 273).

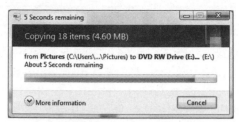

Fig. 4.25 Burning a Folder to CD.

However, should the data you are trying to copy on a CD be large graphical images obtained from, say, a digital camera or a scanner, then it might be a good idea to compress such images before attempting to copy them onto a CD, as discussed below. However, such a problem might not arise if your PC is capable of burning files to a DVD recorder.

Compressing Files and Folders

Compressing files and folders allows you to greatly increase the storage capacity of your hard disc and also increases the amount of data you can copy on a single CD. As an example we will use the first three chapters plus the prelims of this book, which together are 50.1 MB in size, and send them to a compressed folder.

To start the process, we select the files we want to compress, right-click the selection, point to the **Send To** option on the drop-down menu, and click the **Compressed (zipped) Folder** option on the displayed sub-menu, as shown in Fig. 4.26 on the next page.

The created folder has the extension **.zip** and you must retain this when renaming it. Windows automatically gives the folder that contains the zipped files the same name as one of the selected files which, however, you can rename later – remember to keep the **.zip** extension.

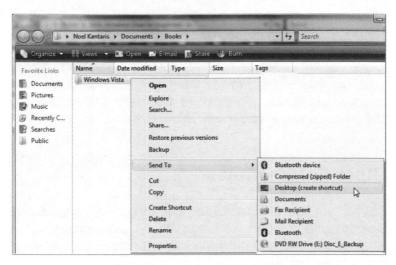

Fig. 4.26 Creating a Zipped Folder.

You can send other files and folders into the compressed folder by dragging them onto it. Selected files are then compressed one at time before they are moved into the folder, while the contents of dragged folders are also compressed.

To find out the size of the folder's contents before and after compression, click the folder to select it (highlight it), right-click it and select **Properties** from the drop-down menu. In our case the size of the folder was 49.8 MB before compression, and 24.2 MB after compression; a large enough compression ratio and worth exploiting.

You can open files and programs in a compressed folder by double-clicking them. To extract a file or folder from a compressed folder, simply drag it to its new location. To extract all files and folders within a compressed folder, right-click the folder and select **Extract All**. In the Extract Wizard you can specify where you want these files and folders to be extracted to.

When you compress files or folders as explained earlier, the original files or folders remain on your hard disc. To remove such files and folders from the originating disc or folder you must delete them. Similarly, when you extract files or folders it leaves a copy of these in the compressed folder. To remove files and folders from a compressed folder you must delete them.

Other Folder Views

So far we have discussed the **Organize** and **Burn** toolbar options when viewing pictures or documents. In what follows, we examine the other toolbar options using the contents of the **Photos** folder, or you could use the **Sample Pictures** folder, as both folders contain the same pictures. Use the **Start**, **Pictures** menu option to open one of the folders by double-clicking its name to display Fig. 4.27 below.

Fig. 4.27 The Photos Folder Displaying the Name Sub-menu.

Clicking the down-arrow against the **Name** box displays a sub-menu, as shown in Fig. 4.27, from which you can choose how to sort your pictures.

Also note that when the **Pictures** (or **Documents**) folder is first opened, and before any item is selected, there are four toolbar options; **Organize**, **Views**, **Slide Show**, and **Burn**, as shown below.

However, when a sub-folder, such as the **Photos** folder is opened, there are only three toolbar options showing.

Next, and as soon you select one or a group of items in a folder or sub-folder, additional options are displayed on the toolbar, as shown in Fig. 4.28 below.

Fig. 4.28 The Photos Folder with Additional Toolbar Options.

The Views Option

In Fig. 4.28 on the previous page, we displayed the contents of the **Photos** folder in **Large Icons**. In Fig. 4.29 below, we display the same contents, but this time in **Tiles**.

Fig. 4.29 The Photos Folder Displayed in Tiles View.

The advantage of displaying items in **Tiles** view is that you can see the size of all the items on the screen at the same time.

The Preview Option

If you now select one image, then click on the down-arrow against the **Preview** toolbar button, you get a list of programs which you can use to edit the selected picture, as shown in Fig. 4.30 on the next page. The list of these programs might be different to you.

Fig. 4.30 The Photos Folder Displaying the Preview Sub-menu.

The most likely program to use here would be the **Windows Photo Gallery** (see Chapter 12, page 234).

The Print Option

Selecting one picture and clicking the **Print** toolbar button, displays the **Print Pictures** window shown below.

Fig. 4.31 The Print Pictures Application.

From here you can select the **Printer** to be used, **Paper size**, and **Quality** of print. You can also choose from a variety of layouts for your pictures. It is perhaps worth spending sometime investigating the various options.

The E-mail Option

Selecting a few pictures and clicking the **E-mail** toolbar button, displays the dialogue box shown in Fig. 4.32.

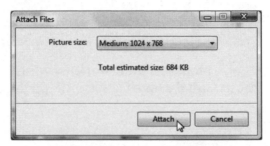

Fig. 4.32 The E-mail Dialogue Box.

In this dialogue box you can choose the **Picture size** of the photos you intend to send as an attachment with your e-mail (more about this shortly). In short, Windows offers to re-size your pictures automatically giving you a choice of five sizes, from 'Smaller' to 'Original'. If the recipient of your e-mail is only using a modem connection to the Internet, then select the 'Smaller' size to save them download time. If your friend is on Broadband, then you could choose 'Medium' or if you are sending only one or two pictures, then you could choose 'Large'.

* * *

In the next chapter we will examine how to use the Control Panel to customise your PC by changing the font size of your screen, install and configure your printer, add hardware and change programs, and examine your PC's System properties.

* * *

5

Customising Windows Vista

You can control your PC primarily from the Windows **Control Panel** which provides a quick and easy way to change the hardware and software settings of your system.

The Windows Control Panel

Fig. 5.1 The Control Panel Menu Option.

To access the **Control Panel**, left-click the **Start** button, then left-click the **Control Panel** entry on the displayed menu, as shown in Fig. 5.1.

This opens the Control Panel window which displays either as shown in Fig. 5.2 (in Category view) or Fig. 5.3 (in Classic view). To see the **Control Panel** in Classic view, left-click the entry **Classic View** on the left panel (pointed to in Fig. 5.2) to display Fig. 5.3. Which view you choose to work with is a matter of personal preference.

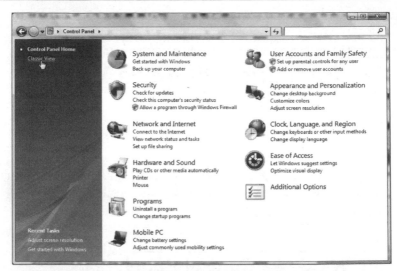

Fig. 5.2 The Control Panel Window in Category View.

Each option within the Category view displays additional options relevant to that category.

Fig. 5.3 The Control Panel Window in Classic View.

From either of these views, you can add new hardware, remove or change programs, change the display type and its resolution, install printers and change their fonts, change the size of the screen fonts, the keyboard repeat rate, the mouse settings, specify regional settings, and access a variety of system administrative tools, to mention but a few.

Further, if your system is connected to the outside world or supports multimedia, then you can also configure these appropriately. All of these features can be used to customise your PC and you should become familiar with them.

Changing your Display

The 3D aspects of Windows Vista require the highest possible screen resolution that your graphics card is capable of delivering. The higher screen resolution, say 1600 x 1200 pixels (picture elements), gives you better text clarity, sharper images, and more items fit on your screen. At lower resolutions (800 x 600 pixels), fewer items fit on the screen, they are larger, but images might appear with jagged edges.

In general, LCD monitors can support higher resolutions than CRT monitors and whether you can increase your screen resolution depends on the size and capability of your monitor and the type of video card installed in your computer.

To see if you can increase your PC's resolution, open the **Control Panel**, and while in Category view, click the **Adjust screen resolution** link, pointed to here, under the **Appearance and Personalization** option.

In the **Display Settings** window, drag the resolution slider towards **High**, as shown in Fig. 5.4.

Fig. 5.4 The Display Settings Window.

For the new settings to take effect, click the **Apply** button, then click **OK** to close the window.

Next, click the **Appearance and Personalization** option link to open an additional window with further choices on this group, as shown in Fig. 5.5 on the next page.

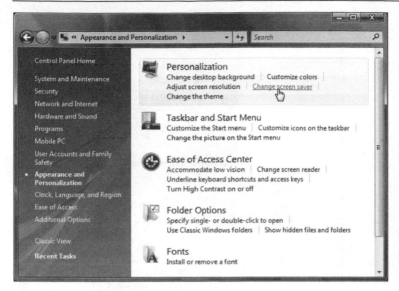

Fig. 5.5 The Display Settings Window.

You might like to explore the other available settings. For example:

- Click the **Change Desktop Background** link to change the background of your desktop, which by default was set to 'img24.jpg'. Each displayed picture has a similar number.

- Click the **Change the theme** link to change the looks of your active windows – best left as it is.

- Click the **Change screen saver** link to select a different screen saver (see Fig. 5.6 on the next page) – you will be able to preview your selection before making a final choice.

It is perhaps worth spending some time here to see the various available effects.

Fig. 5.6 The Screen Saver Settings Window.

On the above window you can also specify how often the screen saver pictures change.

Selecting **My Pictures Premium** option as a screen saver allows you to rotate through the contents of the **Pictures** folder. Left-click the **Settings** button to further select options such as randomise the order of appearance of the pictures, fade them when changing pictures, etc. You can click the **Preview** button to see how it will look on full screen.

For the new settings to take effect, click the **Apply** button, then click **OK** to close the window.

Changing the Font Size of Screen Items

Since increasing resolution makes items appear smaller on screen, we need a way of increasing the size of text and icons without compromising resolution. To achieve this, open **Control Panel**, then click the **Appearance and Personalization** option link to display the screen shown in Fig. 5.5 on page 83.

Next, click the **Personalization** link to display the screen shown in Fig. 5.7 below.

Fig. 5.7 The Personalization Window.

On the left panel of the screen, click the **Adjust font size (DPI)** link. In the displayed DPI Scaling dialogue box select **Large scale (120 DPI)**, then click **Apply**. You will be warned to save all your work before restarting Windows, for the effect to take place. If you don't like it, go through the procedure again, but choose the **Default** option.

Controlling Printers

When you upgraded to Windows Vista your printers should have been installed automatically. If not, click the **Start** button and choose **Printers** from the right column. This opens the **Printers** folder, shown in Fig. 5.8 below.

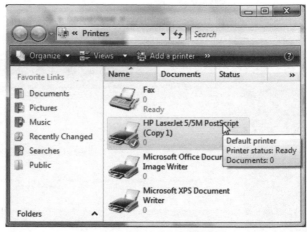

Fig. 5.8 The Printers Folder.

Our **Printers** folder has several printers available for use. The **Add a Printer** toolbar button provides a way of adding new printers. Clicking it displays Fig. 5.9.

Fig. 5.9 The Add a Printer Window.

Windows Vista supports Plug and Play printers which are automatically detected at installation time, or during the boot-up process. You will be prompted for the necessary driver files if they are not already in the Windows directory, these should have been supplied with the new Plug-and-Play printer.

For other situations, the Add a Local Printer option in Fig. 5.9 steps you through the printer installation process, as shown in Fig. 5.10 below.

Fig. 5.10 The Printers Folder.

You could install an additional printer (not connected to your system, but available to you, say, at work), so that you could use the extra fonts available to that printer.

Documents prepared with such a selected printer, could then be printed to file on a recordable compact disc (CD-R), and later printed out on the selected printer at the other location.

Configuring your Printer

To configure your printer, left-click the **Printers** icon in the **Start** menu, select the printer you want to configure, right-click it, and select the **Properties** option in the drop-down menu. This opens the Properties dialogue box for the selected printer.

Fig. 5.11 The Printer Properties Dialogue Box.

From the displayed tabbed dialogue box you can control all the printer's parameters, such as the printer port (or network path), paper and graphics options, built-in fonts, and other device options specific to the printer model. All these settings are fairly self explanatory and as they depend on your printer type, we will leave them to you.

A newly installed printer is automatically set as the default printer, indicated by a tick against it. To change this, select a printer connected to your PC, right-click it, and choose the **Set as Default Printer** option on the displayed shortcut menu.

Once you have installed and configured your printers in Windows they are then available for all your application programs to use. The correct printer is selected usually in one of the application's **File** menu options.

Managing Print Jobs

If you want to find out what exactly is happening while a document or documents are being sent to your printer, double-click the printer icon on the right end of the Task bar, to open its window.

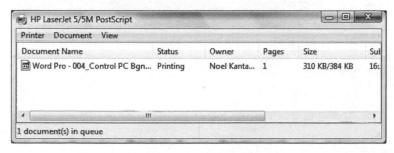

Fig. 5.12 The Print Queue Window.

As shown above, this displays detailed information about the contents of any work actually being printed, or of print jobs that are waiting in the queue. This includes the name of the document, its status and 'owner', when it was added to the print queue, the printing progress and when printing was started.

You can control the printing operation from the **Printer** and **Document** menu options of the **Print Queue** window. Selecting **Printer, Pause Printing** will stop the operation until you make the same selection again. The **Cancel All Documents** option will remove all, or selected, print jobs from the print queue, but it takes time.

The Fax and Scan Printer

Windows Vista includes its own Fax and Scan printer driver which is automatically installed when you upgrade Windows, as shown in Fig. 5.8 on page 86. Double-clicking on the **Fax** icon in the **Printers** window, opens up the **Fax and Scan** window shown in Fig. 5.13 below.

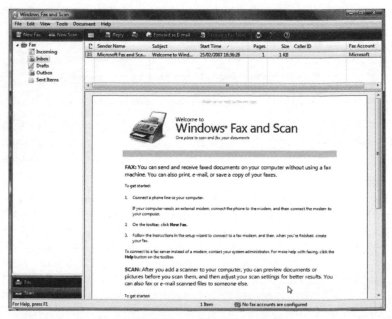

Fig. 5.13 The Fax and Scan Window.

All the printers installed on your system are available to you from within any of the word processing or other applications you might have on your computer so that you can either print a document to your local printer, to a shared printer (if you are connected to a network) or the Fax printer (if you are connected to a phone line). To send and receive Faxes all you need is a fax device, such as a Fax modem – it must support Fax capabilities, not just data standards.

Do try to open the **Fax and Scan** window on your screen so that you can read the instructions for yourself. However, it is important to note that if you are on Broadband, you cannot send a Fax unless you subscribe to a third party provider in which case you send your scanned document as an e-mail attachment and your third party provider sends it on as a Fax. However, this costs money, and is beyond the scope of this book so we will not expand on it.

Adding Hardware to your System

Windows Vista automates the process of adding hardware to your system by including a set of software standards for controlling suitably designed hardware devices.

Plug-and-Play: Windows supports what are known as Plug-and-Play compatible devices. So, when you buy new hardware, make sure that it is Plug-and-Play compatible. Adding such hardware devices to your system is extremely easy, as Windows takes charge and automatically controls all its settings so that it fits in with the rest of the system.

Add New Hardware Wizard: If your new hardware is not Plug-and-Play compatible all is not lost, as there is a very powerful Wizard to help you with their installation. Fit the new hardware before you run the Wizard, as it is just possible that Windows will recognise the change and be able to carry out the configuration by itself.

If the new hardware is not recognised, click the

Hardware and Sound link in the **Control Panel**, shown here, which displays a further screen of available hardware that you can add to your system, as shown in Fig. 5.14.

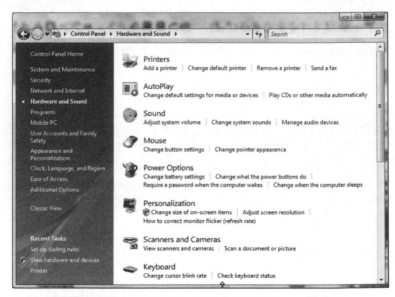

Fig. 5.14 A Selection of Hardware to Add to your System.

All you have to do next is to select the type of hardware you want to add to your system and follow the instructions on screen.

Using Control Panel's Classic View

Sometimes it might be easier to use **Control Panel** in **Classic View** rather than in **Category View**. Adding hardware is a case in point, particularly if you can not find the exact item under the **Hardware and Sound** option.

To display what is shown in Fig. 5.15 below, open **Control Panel** and click the link **Classic View** at the top left of the screen.

Fig. 5.15 A Selection of Hardware to Add to your System.

Double-clicking the **Add Hardware** icon, shown here, starts a powerful Wizard which searches your system for anything new. If the new hardware is not recognised, a list of hardware is displayed and you are asked to specify its type. You might also be asked to insert the CD supplied with the new hardware, if Windows needs to install its driver.

Installing Programs on your PC

Installing programs on your PC is very easy with Windows Vista. Just place the CD or DVD that the software came on in the appropriate drive and Vista will start the installation process automatically.

If the **Setup** program does not start automatically,

then click the **Start** button, type **Run** in the **Start Search** box, shown here and situated just above the **Start** button, and press

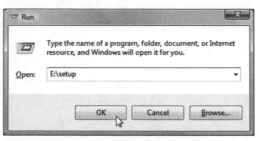

the **Enter** key. This displays the Run box shown in Fig. 5.16.

Next, type in the **Open** box the following:

E:\setup

Fig. 5.16 The Start Dialogue Box.

and click the **OK** button to start the installation of your new software.

Note: In our case the CD/DVD drive is the E: drive, but in your case it could be different.

If you already have versions of programs which worked fine in Windows XP (or earlier versions of Windows), or intend to installed such programs, then you find out that they don't work properly, or don't work at all, use the Program Compatibility Wizard as described at the end of Chapter 13, to correct such misbehaviour. Windows Vista allows such programs to run as if they are running under earlier versions of Windows.

Uninstall or Change a Program

Uninstalling programs or changing an already installed one is very easy with Windows Vista. Double-click the **Programs and Features** icon in the **Classic View** of the **Control Panel** to display a screen similar to the one in Fig. 5.17. What we show here is only the right panel of the screen, and only after selecting a program with a <u>single</u> left-click.

Programs
and Features

Note: Be careful with this application, because double-clicking a program on the list might remove it without further warning!

Uninstall or change a program

To uninstall a program, select it from the list and then click "Uninstall", "Change", or "Repair".

Organize ∨   Views ∨   Uninstall   Change   ?

Name	Publisher	Installed On	Size	
Acronis True Image Home	Acronis	14/02/2007	187 MB	
Adobe Acrobat 7.0.9 Professional	Adobe Systems	06/02/2007	769 MB	
Adobe Flash Player 9 ActiveX	Adobe Systems	06/02/2007		
Adobe Reader 7.0.9	Adobe Systems Incorporated	20/02/2007	65.1 MB	
Advanced Disk Cleaner 4.7	Innovative Solutions	22/02/2007	2.58 MB	
Advanced Uninstaller PRO 2006 - version 7	Innovative Solutions	13/02/2007	19.2 MB	
AVG Free Edition		13/02/2007	28.3 MB	
Conexant HD Audio		06/02/2007	616 KB	
Customer Experience Enhancement	Hewlett-Packard	12/11/2006		
DivX	DivXNetworks, Inc.	06/02/2007	1.54 MB	

Fig. 5.17 Part of the Programs and Features Screen.

After selecting a program the four options, **Organize**, **Views**, **Uninstall**, and **Change** appear on the toolbar. With some programs the toolbar options might change to only three options, while with others a **Repair** option appears in place of **Change**.

Using the option to **Uninstall**, removes all trace of the selected program from your hard disc, although sometimes the folders are left empty on your hard drive.

Checking your Regional Settings

Most Windows application programs use Windows settings to determine how they display and handle time, date, language, numbers, and currency. It is important that you ensure your system was correctly set up during the installation process.

Regional and Language Options

Use the **Start**, **Control Panel** option, then select the **Classic View**, and double-click the **Regional and Language Options** icon, shown here, to open the tabbed dialogue box shown in Fig. 5.18 below.

Fig. 5.18 The Regional Settings Properties Box.

Make sure the various entries are correct. If not, change them by clicking the down arrow to the right of an entry to display a drop-down list and select the most appropriate country and language in the tabbed pages of the dialogue box.

If, in the future, you start getting '$' signs, instead of '£' signs, or commas in numbers where you would expect periods, check your regional settings and click the **Customize this format** button to change the way currency, time, and date display. You will have to click the **Apply** button before any changes become effective.

Changing the Date and Time

Fig. 5.19 Date and Time Properties Dialogue Box.

To the far right of the **Taskbar** you can see displayed the current time. This is the internal clock of your PC which changes automatically between Summer and Winter times. Left-clicking the time icon, opens the Date/Time screen, shown in Fig. 5.19, so that you can make changes, if necessary.

There are other icons to be found at the far right of the **Taskbar** which you might like to investigate. One of these is the **Language** icon, shown here, which when clicked allows you to change between UK and USA English.

System Properties

In the following pages we will look at the **System Properties** to see how well the various hardware parts of our PC are performing when running Windows Vista. To do this, left-click the **Start** button, then right-click (note we've said right-click) the **Computer** entry on the **Start** menu, and select **Properties** from the drop-down sub-menu to display the screen in Fig. 5.20.

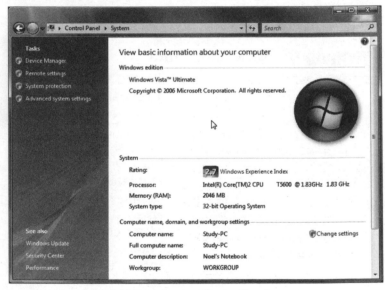

Fig. 5.20 The System Properties Screen.

Next, click the **Windows Experience Index** link to display a screen similar to the one in Fig. 5.21 on the next page.

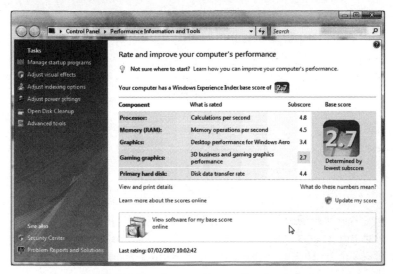

Fig. 5.21 The System Properties Screen.

Here, Windows Vista rates the performance of the various hardware components of one of our computers, and gives it an index number between 1 and 5.9. The overall rating (base score) is the lowest rating of an individual component, not the average. What lets this particular computer down is the Gaming Graphics score, but since no games are ever played on it, it is of no consequence.

In general, a base score of 2 and above indicates that the computer is more or less capable of running everything that Windows Vista can offer. The individual component score is given by this test so that you can see which component of your computer needs upgrading.

* * *

In Chapter 6 we discuss the Windows Paint program. We first introduce Microsoft's Paint, then we show you how to create, view and edit, simple graphics shapes.

* * *

6

The Windows Paint Program

Microsoft **Paint** is a simple graphics 'drawing and painting' program that comes bundled with Windows Vista. So, to all intents and purposes, it is a free painting program that you can use to create, view and edit, simple or complicated graphics or photographs. It can also be used to learn the basics of painting software. Many sophisticated graphics software applications, such as **Paint Shop Pro** or **Photoshop**, use the same basic principles and involve learning how to use the menu and tool bars. This can be far more easily done using **Paint**.

The latest versions of **Paint** let you open and save image files in a much improved range of formats. You can use Windows bitmap files with the **.bmp** extension (24-bit, 256 colour, 16 colour, and monochrome), as well as **.jpg**, **.gif**, **.png**, and .tif files. Older versions of **Paint** cannot open or edit **.gif**, **.png**, and .tif files, and can only open **.jpg** files with a JPEG filter. More about graphic file formats later.

Starting Paint

To start **Paint**, click the **Start** button, hover with mouse pointer over **All Programs**, and select **Accessories** from the displayed menu. Clicking the **Paint** entry starts the program and displays a screen similar to that of Fig. 6.1 on the next page in which we also show a **.jpg** picture file opened.

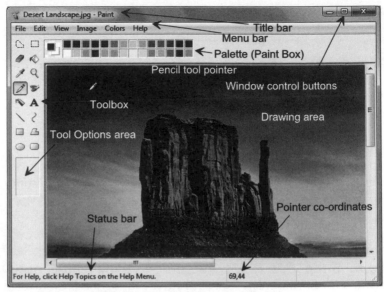

Fig. 6.1 The Paint Opening Screen.

Here we have used the **File**, **Open** command, navigated to the **Pictures** folder and selected the Desert Landscape picture from the **Sample Pictures** sub-folder.

The **Paint** window is divided into a 'Drawing' area (the default size of which depends on your video display), surrounded by the 'Menu' bar at the top, the 'Palette' below it, the 'Options' area at the middle-left side, with the 'Toolbox' above it.

The Paint Toolbox

The drawing area is where you create your drawings with the help of various tools from the Toolbox. Note that the pencil tool is always selected when you start **Paint**, as shown above.

To select a tool, simply point to it and click. Several of them have extra functions you can also select in the Options area. Some tools can work with either of the current foreground or background colours – dragging the tool with the left mouse button uses the foreground colour and with the right one the background colour.

More detail of the Toolbox functions is listed below.

Tool	*Function*
Free-Form Select	Used to cut out an irregular-shaped area of a picture, with either an opaque or transparent background, which can then be dragged to another part of the drawing, or manipulated using the **Edit** menu commands.
Select	Used to cut out a rectangular-shaped area of a picture, with either an opaque or transparent background, which can then be dragged to another part of the drawing, or manipulated using the **Edit** menu commands.
Eraser/Color Eraser	Used to change the selected foreground colours under the eraser icon to a background colour, or automatically change every occurrence of one colour in the drawing area to another.
Fill With Color	Used to fill in any closed shape or area with the current foreground or background colour.

Pick Color

Used to set the foreground or background colour to that at the pointer.

Magnifier

Used to zoom the image to different magnifications. Choose from 1x, 2x, 6x or 8x magnification in the options area.

Pencil

Used to draw freehand lines in either the foreground or background colour.

Brush

Used to draw freehand lines with a selection of tools and line thickness in the options area.

Airbrush

Used to produce one of three available circular sprays in foreground or background colours.

Text

Used to add text of different fonts, sizes and attributes in the current foreground colour, with either an opaque or transparent background.

Line

Used to draw straight lines between two points in the current foreground or background colour and drawing width.

Curve

Used to draw curved lines in the current colours and drawing width.

Rectangle

Used to draw hollow and filled rectangles (or squares with the

Shift key depressed), in the current colours and width.

Polygon

Used to draw hollow and filled triangles and other polygon shapes, in the current colours and drawing width.

Ellipse

Used to draw hollow and filled ellipses (or circles with the **Shift** key depressed), in the current colours and drawing width.

Rounded Rectangle

Used to draw hollow and filled rectangles (or squares with the **Shift** key depressed), with rounded corners, in the current colours and width.

Tool Options

When a tool is selected, options may appear in the Tool Options area below the tool buttons, shown in Fig. 6.1. These options provide a way to customise the tools. The options vary according to which tool you are using.

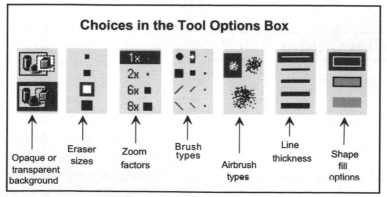

Fig. 6.2 The Various Tool Options.

As shown in Fig. 6.2, the various options include; line thickness, airbrush density, size and shape of the paintbrush or whether a shape is to be filled or hollow. Some tools have no options, and when they are active (either selected or in use) the Tool Options area remains blank.

Perhaps the options that need more explanation are the two, shown here, that control whether the background of a selection is opaque or transparent. These become available when the two Selection tools and the Text tool are active. We show here the opaque background option selected; the top of the two.

When you have white as your background colour (the colour selected by the right mouse button) and have chosen the transparent option, anything you select from a picture with a white background can be pasted without a rectangle of white surrounding it.

If the item you want to select is sitting on a background of a colour other than white, clicking your right button on that colour will make it possible for you to select the item without its background. Hopefully this will become clearer a little later on.

The Colour Palette

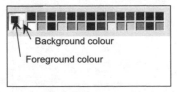

Fig. 6.3 The Paint Palette.

At the top of the **Paint** window is the colour palette, as shown in Fig. 6.3.

The two squares pointed to here show the active colours which are presently in use. When you click on a colour in the palette with the left mouse button, that colour will be set as the primary or foreground colour, here shown as black. The colour you click on with the right mouse button will be the secondary or background colour, here shown as white.

The Colour Palette shows the conventional 28 colours that are most used in Windows computing. You can very easily customise the palette though, by double-clicking on any colour, which opens the Edit Colors box shown on the left in Fig. 6.4 below.

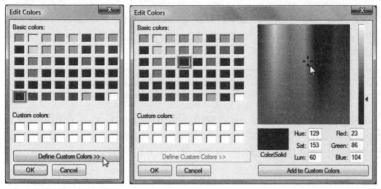

Fig. 6.4 Selecting Custom Colours in the Edit Colors box.

To add colours to the colour palette, click on the **Define Custom Colors>>** button and the window will be enlarged to include a fairly sophisticated colour picker, as shown on the right of Fig. 6.4.

As you move the cursor over the matrix panel, the numerical boxes below display the colour value in terms of **Hue**, **Sat**uration and **Lum**inosity (H,S and L in many graphics programs), and in terms of **Red**, **Green** and **Blue** (R, G and B) content. When you click the colour you want, these values become 'fixed' and that colour is placed in the **Color|Solid** box. Clicking the **Add to Custom Colors** button will add the colour to the **Custom Colors** pane. They can then be selected for use in the main colour palette.

If you know the RGB or HSL value of the colour you want to use, you can enter their values into the individual boxes. Clicking the **OK** button closes the Edit Color dialogue box.

The Status Bar

At the bottom of the **Paint** window is the Status Bar, which gives information on what you are doing, where your mouse pointer is (in this case 32,107 – 32 pixels from the left margin and 107 pixels from the top margin), and the size of a selection or shape (in this case 80x44 – 80 pixels wide by 44 pixels height).

Fig. 6.5 The Status Bar Information.

When you move the mouse pointer over a tool button or a sub-menu item, a brief description of the item is displayed on the Status Bar.

The Menu Bar

One difference between **Paint** and its more powerful and more expensive alternatives, like **Paint Shop Pro** or **Photoshop**, is that **Paint** does not have tool bars of icons that you can click to carry out menu actions. With **Paint** you have to use menu commands, or keyboard shortcut keystrokes, to carry out all actions except those of actually drawing or painting. With that in mind we will look at all of the menu bar options, shown in Fig. 6.6 after pressing the **Alt** key .

Fig. 6.6 The Paint Menu Bar.

The File Menu

The File Menu is where you will find commands that affect the file you are working on in its most basic aspects. This is where you would go to create a new file, open a file, save a file, or print a file. Its sub-menu options have the following functions:

New – creates a new, blank (white) image file.

Open – displays the Open dialogue box for you to open an image file; one at a time. If you try to open a second file, the first file will be closed automatically.

Save – saves the current file to disc, without opening a dialogue box.

Save As – also lets you save the current file, but allows you to change its name in the Save As dialogue box.

From Scanner or Camera – lets you load an image into Paint from a digital camera or scanner, as long as one is connected and active.

Print Preview – displays the image on screen as it will appear when it is printed out on paper.

Page Setup – displays options for setting up how Paint will print an image.

Print – opens the Print dialogue box, so that you can Print the current image to paper.

Send – opens your e-mail program with the current file set as an attachment, so that you can send your work to grandma.

Set As Background – lets you make the current picture the background image on your Windows desktop. You can choose for it to be **Centered** or **Stretched**.

Exit – lets you save the current file and exits the program.

The Edit Menu

This menu is where you will find many of the commands for working within an image to make any editing changes you require. Its sub-menu options have the following functions:

Undo – is probably the most important command to remember. It undoes, or removes, up to the last three changes you made to the current image.

Repeat – reverses the last Undo command.

Cut – removes a selected section from the current image, and places it on the Windows clipboard.

Copy – places the selected portion of the image onto the clipboard, but it does not remove it from the image.

Paste – adds the contents of the clipboard back into the image, where you can move it around before deselecting it.

Clear Selection – deletes any selected items from the current image.

Select All – selects the entire image so that you can then use another command on it.

Copy To – opens the Copy To dialogue box and lets you save the current selection as a separate file.

Paste From – opens the Paste From dialogue box so that you can paste the contents of a separate file into the currently active Paint file.

The View Menu

If you can't see the Tool Box, Color Box, or Status Bar in your Paint window, go into the View menu and make sure a check mark appears next to each option.

Tool Box, **Color Box**, **Status Bar** and **Text Toolbar** – all let you toggle whether the feature will be displayed in the Paint window.

Zoom – opens a sub-menu that lets you magnify the current image display, show a grid on it, and open a separate Thumbnail window showing the image. The latter can be useful to show the whole image when you are working at high magnification or zoom levels.

View Bitmap – lets you see the whole image full screen and at normal size.

The Image Menu

You can use the tools in this menu to alter your image or selection in a number of interesting and useful ways.

Flip/Rotate – opens the Flip and Rotate dialogue box which lets you flip the selection (or whole image) vertically or horizontally (to make a mirror image), or to rotate it in the same plane through 90° increments (90°, 180°, and 270°).

Resize/Skew – opens the Resize and Skew box. The **Resize** option allows you to change the proportions of the selection. The **Skew** option affects opposite edges. A horizontal skew might shift the top of the image to the right while the bottom of the image stretches to the left.

Crop – allows you to crop an image.

Invert Colors – gives an effect similar to a photographic negative. We have not found much use for this!

Attributes – opens the Attributes box. This gives some information on the image file and lets you change the basic image attributes such as **Width** and **Height** (in pixels, inches, or cm), and **Colors**.

Clear Image – wipes out the image contents, leaving you with a blank file with the same image dimensions.

Draw Opaque – works with the selection process. If this option is unchecked, any background colour (the default being white) in a selection will be treated as transparent and can be seen by moving it over other areas of the image. You should be able to see those areas peeking through the selection. If the option is unchecked, the background colour will remain opaque when the selection is moved about in the image.

The Colors Menu

This menu only has one option in it, which is:

Edit Colors – allows you to open the Edit Colors box shown previously in Fig. 6.4. This lets you select different colours for the main palette, or Color Box. You can also add colours to the palette in a colour picker.

The Help Menu

This menu only has two options in it, which are:.

Help Topics – opens the Help and Support Windows Vista screen and gives you instant help on using Paint.

About Paint – opens the copyright box, with information on the version of Paint and the registered user.

Now that we have gone over the basics of the program it is time to look at how to actually use it. Its main functions are:

- To create and edit drawings, view and simply edit photos obtained from a digital camera or scanner.

- To send images using e-mail and set pictures as your desktop background.

Electronic Painting

With Paint you can draw and paint on the screen in the same manner as an artist works on paper or canvas. The tools used are actually very similar; brushes, airbrushes and erasers. The techniques though are a little different and for the first-timer it takes a little getting used to.

Before you start drawing, you may need to set the size of the image you want using the **Image**, **Attributes** menu command.

Using the Paint Tools

Most of the tools in the Paint Toolbox are quite easy and straightforward to use. To select a tool, point to it and click the left mouse button, which depresses its icon in the Toolbox. To use it, you move the pointer to a suitable position within the drawing area and drag the tool around to accomplish the required task. Sounds very artistic, doesn't it?

With most of the Toolbox options, dragging with the left mouse button uses the active foreground colour, and with the right button the active background colour. Releasing the mouse button stops the action being performed. If you make a mistake, you can select the **Edit, Undo** command from the menu bar (or **Ctrl+Z**) up to three times, to cancel the last action you carried out.

As you select a tool, you are given a choice within the Tools Options area of shapes or sizes of the tool you have selected. For example, in Fig. 6.7 we show the choice of brushes available to you when you select the **Brush** tool. Here, the first brush type is active (top left one in the box) and the mouse pointer ᛫᛫᛫ changes to show which brush you are working with.

Fig. 6.7 Using the Brush.

To complete this discussion, we need to describe how to use the **Curve**, **Polygon** tools, and the three shape tools, **Rectangle**, **Ellipse** and **Rounded Rectangle**. These tools differ slightly from the rest. For example:

To draw a curve, first click the **Curve** toolbar icon, choose a line thickness in the options box, left-click the pointer in the required starting position within the drawing area, then press the left mouse button to anchor the beginning of the curve and move the mouse to the required end of the eventual curve and release it. A 'flexible' line in the current foreground colour will be produced between the two points. Next, click the mouse button away from the line and drag it around the window, which causes the line to curve as you move the pointer. When you are happy with the produced curvature, release the mouse button.

To draw a polygon, place the Polygon pointer in the required starting point in the drawing area, left-click and drag the mouse to the required end of the first side of the polygon and release it. A line in the foreground colour is produced between the two points. Next, continue adding sides to the polygon in this way until you complete it, at which point you should double-click the mouse button.

The other three shape tools, **Rectangle**, **Ellipse** and **Rounded Rectangle** all behave the same as each other, but obviously produce different shapes. They all have the same three options in the Options Box; outline, foreground colour filled with the background colour, and solid in the foreground colour.

Note: The thickness of the outline shapes of polygons, rectangles and ellipses, is set by the last choice made for **Line** thickness. If the border is not the right thickness, choose a different one, then click the shape tool again.

The Select Tool

 This is one of the two selection tools in Paint. You use it to make rectangular selections of the current image. You can do several things with a selection.

• Move the selection contents about the image by dragging it with the ✛ pointer.

• **Copy** and **Paste** it to a different part of the drawing, or to a different drawing.

• Move it from one part of a drawing to another, using the **Cut** and **Paste** commands.

• Delete an area of the image it covers with the **Delete** key.

• Use the selection as a paint brush.

To make a selection you click the **Select** button, position the ┼ pointer at the top left corner of the area, and drag across the part of the image you want to select. While dragging, the selection is shown as a black dashed rectangle. When you release the mouse button, this rectangle turns to blue and handles are placed at each corner and the middle of each side, as shown in Fig. 6.8. If you click anywhere outside the selection it will be cancelled.

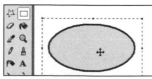

Fig. 6.8 An Active Selection.

Unlike many other graphics programs, you can actually adjust the selection after it is made, by placing the pointer over one of the handles and dragging, as shown in Fig. 6.9 on the next page.

Dragging the ↖ pointer over the corner handles lets you make the whole selection area bigger or smaller, while dragging the ↕ pointer over a side handle lets you adjust the position of that side.

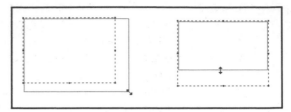

Fig. 6.9 Re-sizing a Selection after it has been Made

When you put your cursor anywhere inside the selection area, it changes to a ✛ shape. If you click the right mouse button, a menu of available options is opened. These give you quick access to the menu commands that are available to you for manipulating the selection.

Using the left mouse button and the ✛ pointer you can also drag the selection to where you want on the image. There are two things to think about when moving a selection. The first is the palette background colour, the one used by the right mouse button drawing actions. As you move a selection, the vacated area will be filled with that colour, so make sure that the palette background colour is the same as the background of your picture. If necessary, use **Ctrl+Z** to undo the action, re-set the background colour and start again.

The other consideration is **transparency**. You may want to move the selection just as it is, a rectangular shape with maybe a lot of white background. But often you will only want to move what you've drawn, in which case the background white needs to be transparent. The two icons shown here that appear in the Options Box when you click on the **Select** tool, control transparency. With the bottom icon highlighted, as shown here, the selection will be transparent. With the top icon highlighted it will be opaque and the whole rectangular area will be selected.

To copy a selection and place the copy elsewhere in the image, place the ✛ pointer inside the selection rectangle (Fig. 6.10a) and check that transparency is set the way you want it. Then with the **Ctrl** key depressed, drag the selection to the place where you want the copy and click (Fig. 6.10b). You can carry on doing this as long as you keep the **Ctrl** key depressed. Each time you click you leave a copy. The last copy (Fig. 6.10c) was also flipped horizontally using the **Image Flip/Rotate** menu command.

Fig. 6.10 The Action of Copying a Selection.

In our example above, we have used a Clip Art image that came with a Microsoft application, but it works with any type of image.

Adding Text to a Drawing

Adding text to a drawing is easy. Simply choose the foreground colour for the text, then select the **Text** tool from the Toolbox and select opaque or transparent from the options box.

Next, click the pointer on the working area to open the text box, drag it to the correct size, type the text, and in the displayed Fonts toolbar select the font and point size.

When you are happy with the text, click outside the text box to paste it in the drawing and close the toolbar. However, it is possible to move a text box before pasting by hovering the cursor exactly over the dashed selection line (Fig. 6.10c) until the ⃗ arrow pointer appears, then press the left mouse button and drag the text box to a new position.

Also, before you click outside the text box and paste the text into the picture, check your transparency icons in the Options Box. If you wanted the text pasted on a rectangular background so that it stands out from the rest of the picture, have the top icon highlighted. If you want the text without a background, choose the lower icon.

While the Fonts toolbar is open you can change any of its options, or use the palette, and see the entered text change straight away. In the future, as long as the **Text Toolbar** option is ticked in the **View** menu, the Fonts toolbar will open whenever you start to enter text.

Saving Images

In Paint the procedure for saving your images as files is the same as with most other Windows programs. You use the **File, Save** command, or **Ctrl+S**, to save existing files when you want the file format to be preserved, and the **File, Save As** command to save new files or when you want to save in a different format.

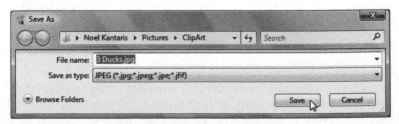

Fig. 6.11 The Save As Dialogue Box.

Desktop Background Image

If you are so happy with your current **Paint** drawing or photograph that you want to look at it every time your PC is running, use one of the **File**, **Set As Background** menu commands. **Centered** puts the image in the middle of your desktop and **Tiled** repeats it over the screen as a sort of collage.

Paint and the Internet

Even with the Internet, Paint can be a useful tool. We show here the two main ways you can use it. One involves sending your picture or drawing to a distant friend, and the other getting pictures from your favourite Web sites.

Sending an Image with E-mail

To send the current image in Paint as an e-mail attachment (more about this later), just use the **File**, **Send** command. This opens your default e-mail program ready for you to enter the receiver's address and your message. It couldn't be easier, but don't forget to make sure the file is not too large. Otherwise you may tie up your recipient's connection for too long. In fact some e-mail hosts don't allow very large files to be sent as attachments.

Copying from a Web Page

Often while browsing our favourite Web sites we find a picture that is just right for something we have in mind. No problem, apart from copyright of course, so be on your guard.

To copy a picture, right-click the image and select **Copy** from the drop-down menu, as shown in Fig. 6.12 below.

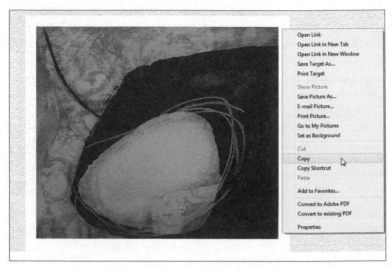

Fig. 6.12 Getting a Picture from a Web Page.

This places the image on the Windows **Clipboard**. You could, of course, have chosen the **Save Picture As** option and saved the picture file on your hard disc. But we want to put it straight into **Paint**, so that it can be changed before it is saved.

Without doing any more editing operations, go to the open Paint window and use the **Edit**, **Paste** menu command, or the **Ctrl+V** keyboard shortcut. Both of these commands paste the clipboard contents into **Paint**, as show in Fig. 6.13 on the next page.

What we have done here is to copy the two images into **Paint**. Note that when an image is pasted, any previous selections are closed and a new selection marquee is placed around the new pasting, so that you can move it round the canvas as you like. We have placed the new image partially on top of that in Fig. 6.10.

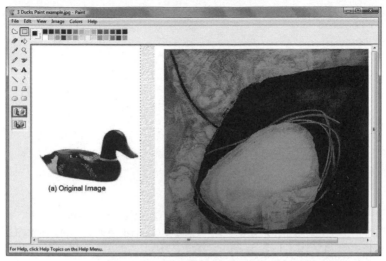

Fig. 6.13 Pasting Images into Paint.

What you do with your new image is up to you, but please don't forget that someone has the copyright for it. If you want to use it, remember to get the permission of the original owner.

* * *

In Chapter 7 we discuss how to control information. We first introduce Microsoft's WordPad and show you how to create, format, save and print documents, and embed and link graphics to a document, before discussing Microsoft's Notepad.

* * *

7

Controlling Information

When you are using one of Windows Vista's applications, you will invariably come across a **Readme.txt** file which contains last minute information not available in printed form in the User Guides. Vendors create such text files which can be read by either the **Notepad** or **WordPad** accessories. What follows will show you how to read such files, print them, or copy them onto the **Clipboard**, so that you can transfer the information into another package.

Microsoft's WordPad

WordPad supports mainly text document formats with file extensions **.txt** and **.rtf**, but has no pagination features. It is a useful accessory for writing and reading simple documents or memos.

To access **WordPad**, click the **Start** button, select **All Programs**, **Accessories**, and click the **WordPad** icon, shown here.

The WordPad Window

When you open **WordPad**, it displays an application window similar to the one in Fig. 7.1 on the next page.

The top line of the **WordPad** window is the 'Title' bar which contains the name of the document, and if this bar is dragged with the mouse the window can be moved around the screen. Also, just like any other window, its size can be changed by dragging any of its four sides in the required direction.

The various areas of the **WordPad** window have the following functions:

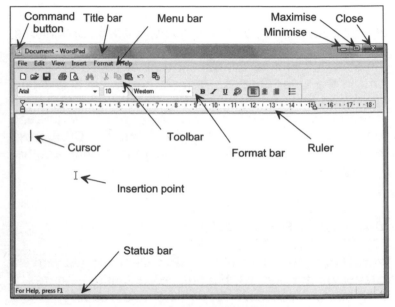

Fig. 7.1 The WordPad Window.

The second line of the window displays the 'Menu' bar which allows access to the following sub menus:

    File   Edit   View   Insert   Format   Help

The sub-menus are accessed either with your mouse, or by pressing the Alt key which underlines one letter per menu option. Typing the underlined letter accesses the sub-menu of that menu command.

The Toolbar

As with most Windows applications, the toolbar contains a set of icon buttons that you click to carry out some of the more common menu functions. The actions of each icon are outlined in Fig. 7.2 below.

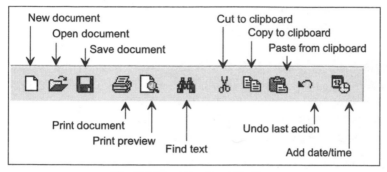

Fig. 7.2 The WordPad Toolbar.

The Format Bar

WordPad has an extra bar of icons that are used to more easily control the format of text in a document.

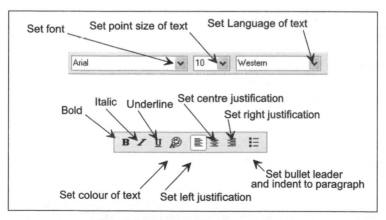

Fig. 7.3 The WordPad Format Bar.

Entering Text

In order to illustrate some of **WordPad**'s capabilities, you need to have a short text at hand. We suggest you type the memo below into a new document. At this stage, don't worry if the length of the lines below differ from those on your display.

As you type in text, any time you want to force a new line, or paragraph, just press the **Enter** key. While typing within a paragraph, **WordPad** sorts out line lengths automatically (known as 'word wrap'), without you having to press any keys to move to a new line.

MEMO TO PC USERS
Networked Computers
The microcomputers in the Data Processing room are a mixture of IBM compatible PCs with Pentium processors running at various speeds. Some have the old 3.5" floppy drives of 1.44MB capacity, most also have CD-ROM drives, while the latest machines are equipped with DVD drives of 4.7GB capacity. The PCs are connected to various printers via a network; the Laser printers available giving best output.

The computer you are using will have at least a 100 GB capacity hard disc on which a number of software programs, including the latest version of Windows, have been installed. To make life easier, the hard disc is highly structured with each program installed in a separate folder.

Fig. 7.4 The WordPad Open Dialogue Box.

Opening a WordPad Document

In you prefer to use your own document, then left-click the **Open** button on **WordPad**'s toolbar, shown here, and select one from the displayed Open dialogue box.

You can use the Open dialogue box to open documents that might have been created by different applications, as shown on the drop-down list against **Files of type**, or documents that are kept in different locations. For example, you can open a document which might be on your computer's hard disc, or on a network drive that you have a connection to.

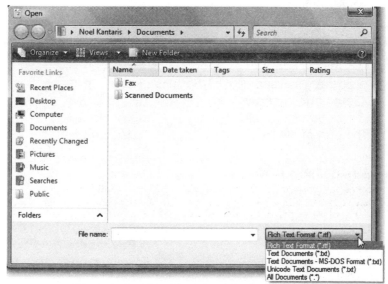

Fig. 7.5 The WordPad Open Dialogue Box.

Having selected a drive and folder within which your document was saved, select its filename and click the **Open** button on the dialogue box.

WordPad can read (and write) five types of file formats; Word for Windows (**.doc**) files, but you have to select the **All Documents** (*.*) file type to see such filenames – more about saving **.doc** files shortly, Rich Text Format (**.rtf**) files, Text Document (**.txt** – both ANSI and ASCII formats), Text Document – MS-DOS Format (**.txt**) files, and Unicode Text Document (**.txt**) files.

Moving Around a WordPad Document

You can move the cursor around a document with the mouse, the normal direction keys, and with key combinations, the most useful of which are listed below.

To move	Press
Left one character	⇐
Right one character	⇒
Up one line	⇑
Down one line	⇓
To beginning of line	Home
To end of line	End
Up one window	Page Up
Down one window	Page Down
To beginning of file	Ctrl+Home
To end of file	Ctrl+End

Saving to a File

To save a document, click the **Save** toolbar icon, shown here, or use the **File, Save** command. A dialogue box appears on the screen with the cursor in the

Fig. 7.6 The Save As Dialogue Box.

File name field box waiting for you to type a name. You can select a drive or a folder, other than the one displayed.

There are four formatting choices in the **Save as type** box when first saving a **WordPad** document. These are the three text (**.txt**) types, and the Rich Text Format (**.rtf**) type.

You can also save a document in Word for Windows (**.doc**) format by including the extension at the end of the filename within the **File name** box. However, such saved files can only be read by Microsoft Word! It is therefore preferable to save your work in Rich Text Format (**.rtf**) format.

To save your document in the future with a different name use the **File**, **Save As** menu command.

Document Editing

For small deletions, such as letters or words, the easiest way is to use the **Delete** or **BkSp** keys. With the **Delete** key, position the cursor on the first letter you want to remove and press **Delete**; the letter is deleted and the following text moves one space to the left. With the **BkSp** key, position the cursor immediately to the right of the character to be deleted and press **BkSp**; the cursor moves one space to the left pulling the rest of the line with it and overwriting the character to be deleted. Note that the difference between the two is that with **Delete** the cursor does not move at all.

Text editing is usually carried out in the insert mode. Any characters typed will be inserted at the cursor location and the following text will be pushed to the right, and down. Pressing the **Insert** key will change to Overstrike mode, which causes entered text to overwrite any existing text at the cursor.

When larger scale editing is needed, use the **Cut**, **Copy** and **Paste** operations; the text to be altered must be 'selected' before these operations can be carried out. These functions are then available when the **Edit** sub-menu is activated, or toolbar icons are used.

Selecting Text

The procedure in **WordPad**, as in all Windows applications, is that before any operation such as formatting or editing can be carried out on text, you first select the text to be altered. Selected text is highlighted on the screen. This can be carried out in several ways:

a.   **Using the keyboard**; position the cursor on the first character to be selected, hold down the **Shift** key while using the direction keys to highlight the required text, then release the **Shift** key. Navigational key combinations can also be used with the **Shift** key to highlight blocks of text.

b.   **With the mouse**; click the left mouse button at the beginning of the block and drag the cursor across the block so that the desired text is highlighted, then release the mouse button. To select a word, double-click in the word, to select a larger block, place the cursor at the beginning of the block, and with the **Shift** key depressed, move the mouse pointer to the end of the desired block, and click the left mouse button.

Using the 'selection area' and a mouse; place the mouse pointer in the left margin area of the **WordPad** window where it changes to a right slanting arrow, and click the left mouse button once to select the current line, twice to select the current paragraph, or three times to select the whole document.

Try out all these methods and find out the one you are most comfortable with.

Copying Blocks of Text

Once text has been selected it can be copied to another location in your present document, to another **WordPad** document, or to another Windows application. As with most of the editing and formatting operations there are many ways of doing this.

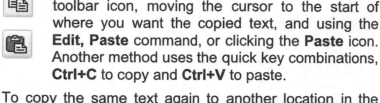

The first is by using the **Edit, Copy** command sequence from the menu, or clicking the **Copy** toolbar icon, moving the cursor to the start of where you want the copied text, and using the **Edit, Paste** command, or clicking the **Paste** icon. Another method uses the quick key combinations, **Ctrl+C** to copy and **Ctrl+V** to paste.

To copy the same text again to another location in the document, move the cursor to the new location and paste it there with either of the above methods.

Drag and Drop – Maybe the easiest way to copy selected text, or an object such as a graphic, is to drag it with the left mouse button and the **Ctrl** key both depressed and to release the mouse button when the vertical line that follows the pointer is at the required destination.

As you get used to Windows application packages you will be able to decide which of these methods is best for you.

Moving Blocks of Text

Selected text can also be moved, in which case it is deleted in its original location. Use the **Edit, Cut**, command, or the **Ctrl+X** keyboard shortcut, or click the **Cut** icon, move the cursor to the required new location and then use the **Edit**, **Paste** command, **Ctrl+V**, or click the **Paste** icon.

The moved text will be placed at the cursor location and will force any existing text to make room for it. This operation can be cancelled by simply pressing **Esc**.

Drag and Drop – Selected text, or an object such as a graphic, can be moved by dragging it with the left mouse button depressed and releasing the button when the vertical line that follows the mouse pointer is at the required destination.

Deleting Blocks of Text

When text is deleted it is removed from the document. With **WordPad** any selected text can be deleted with the **Edit**, **Cut** command, or by simply pressing the **Delete** key. However, using **Edit**, **Cut** (or **Ctrl+X**) places the text on the Windows clipboard and allows you to use the **Edit**, **Paste** (or **Ctrl+V**) command, while using the **Delete** key does not.

The Undo Command

As text is lost with the delete command you should use it with caution, but if you do make a mistake all is not lost as long as you act immediately. The **Edit**, **Undo** command (or **Ctrl+Z**), or clicking the **Undo** toolbar button, reverses your most recent action, so you need to use it before carrying out any further operations.

Finding and Changing Text

WordPad allows you to search for specified text, or character combinations. In the **Find** mode it will highlight each occurrence in turn so that you can carry out some action on it. In the **Replace** mode you specify what replacement is to be carried out.

For example, in a long memo you may decide to replace every occurrence of the word 'program' with the word 'programme'. To do this, first go to the beginning of the document, as searches operate in a forward direction, then choose the **Edit**, **Replace** menu command to open a dialogue box, like the one shown in Fig. 7.7.

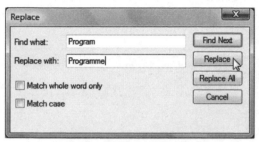

Fig. 7.7 The Replace Dialogue Box.

You type what you want to search for in the **Find what** box. You can then specify whether you want to **Match whole word only**, and whether to **Match case**, (upper or lower case) by check-marking the appropriate boxes. Type the replacement word in the **Replace with** box, and then make a selection from one of the four buttons provided. Selecting **Replace** requires you to manually confirm each replacement, whilst selecting **Replace All** will replace all occurrences of the word automatically.

Formatting your Work

When working with text files you cannot format your documents, but in Microsoft Word, or RTF modes, you can. Such formatting can involve the appearance of individual characters or words, and the indentation, addition of bullet leaders and the alignment of paragraphs. These functions are carried out in **WordPad** from the **Format** menu options or from the Format bar.

To activate the latter, if it is not already activated, use the **View** command and click the **Format Bar** option, as shown in Fig. 7.8.

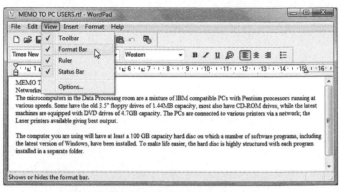

Fig. 7.8 Activating the Formatting Bar.

As an example of some of the formatting options, we have carried out a few changes to the **MEMO TO PC USERS.rtf** document created earlier. We used the **Save As** command to save the document as an **RTF** type file on our hard drive, so that we could carry out certain formatting commands (such as justification) which are not available to a **TXT** type file.

We then highlighted the two title lines, and changed

their point size to 16, then emboldened them and centre justified them by clicking appropriate format bar options.

The rest of the document was selected and its font changed from Courier New to **Arial** by choosing the font type from the drop-down list shown in Fig. 7.9.

Fig. 7.9 The Font List.

Finally, the date was then added below the second line of
the title by clicking the **Date/Time** icon on the
toolbar and choosing the date format required.
The result is shown in Fig. 7.10.

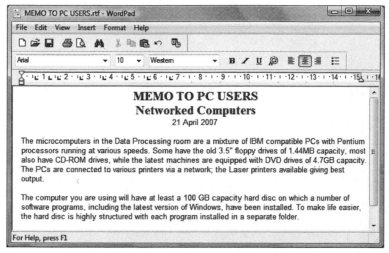

Fig. 7.10 The Display of a Formatted Document.

Formatting Lists

It is easy to create a bulleted list in **WordPad**. Just type
the list as a series of separate lines, highlight them
all and use the **Format**, **Bullet Style** menu
command, or click the **Bullets** toolbar button, as
shown in Fig. 7.11 on the next page.

This places bullets in front of each list item. Boring I
can hear you saying, but wait there is more. With the list
still selected try pressing the **Ctrl+Shift+L** key
combination. The bullets will change to numbers.

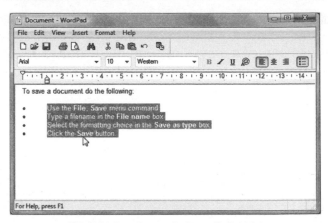

Fig. 7.11 Creating an Ordinary Bullet List.

In fact you can cycle through six types of bullet 'styles' by continuously using the **Ctrl+Shift+L** key combination. These include alphabetical list markers, ordinary numbers and Roman numerals, as shown in Fig. 7.12. This feature does not seem to be mentioned anywhere by Microsoft.

•	1.	a.	A.	i.	I.
•	2.	b.	B.	ii.	II.
•	3.	c.	C.	iii.	III.
•	4.	d.	D.	iv.	IV.

Fig. 7.12 Available Bullet Styles in WordPad.

The Ruler

The ruler is activated/deactivated by using the **View**, **Ruler** command. The Ruler displays at the top of the text area of the **WordPad** window (see Fig. 7.11), and lets you set and see Tab points for your text, or visually change the left and right margins, (the empty space to the left and right of the text area) of your document.

Setting your own tabs is easy by clicking within the ruler where you want to set the tab. Tabs can be moved within the ruler by dragging them with the mouse to a new position, or removed by simply dragging them off the ruler. Default tab settings do not show on the ruler, but custom tabs do.

Printing Documents

As long as your printer has been properly installed and configured, you should have no problems printing your document from the **WordPad** application.

Setting up your Page

Before attempting to print, make sure that **WordPad** is set to the same page size as the paper you plan to use. To do this, use the **File**, **Page Setup** menu command to open the dialogue box shown in Fig. 7.13. From here you can control the paper **Size** and **Source**, the size of all the **Margins** around the edge of the sheet, and the **Orientation** of the paper. The **Printer** button lets you select between different

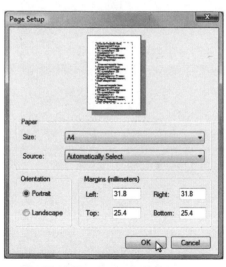

Fig. 7.13 The Page Setup Screen.

printers, including network printers (if you are connected to any), and set their properties.

Print Preview

Before actually committing yourself and printing your document to paper, it is always best to look at a Preview on the screen. This can save both your paper and printer toner or cartridge bills.

To preview the current document and settings, either click the Print Preview icon on the toolbar, or use the **File, Print Preview** menu command to display the following screen.

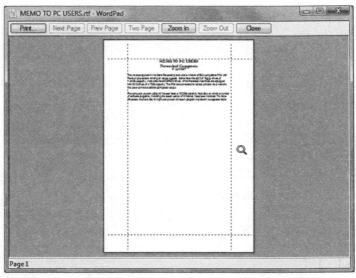

Fig. 7.14 The Print Preview Screen.

The preview screen, shown above, is the only place in **WordPad** that you can actually see your document's pagination, and then you have no control over it! A dreadful omission, but perhaps intentional, to make sure everyone buys Microsoft Word instead!

To zoom in on the document, just click the pointer on it, or use the **Zoom In** button. When you are happy your document is perfect, press the **Print** button.

Embedding a Graphic into WordPad

Embedding a graphic into WordPad is similar to copying, but with the important advantage that you can actually edit an embedded object from within WordPad.

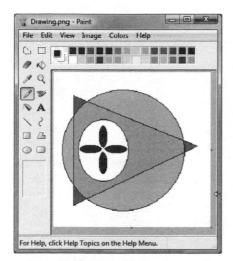

Fig. 7.15 Creating a Graphic in Paint.

To embed a Paint image, first create it in Paint (we created the object shown in Fig. 7.15 in order to illustrate the process), then save it as a **.png** file. Next, start **WordPad**, open the letter or memo you want to embed a graphic into (or just use an empty document), place the cursor where you want to embed it, and press the **Enter** key twice to make some room.

Now from the WordPad menu bar, use the **Insert, Object** command which displays the Insert Object dialogue box shown in Fig. 7.16. Click the **Create from**

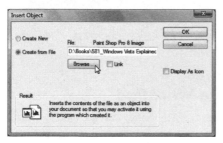

Fig. 7.16 The Insert Object Box.

File radio button, **Browse** to locate your **.png** drawing, and press **OK** to place the selected graphic into the **WordPad** document, as shown in Fig. 7.17 on the next page.

Here we have embedded the graphic in the current **WordPad** document, then changed its size and shape to our liking. If you double-click the graphic, the WordPad window will change to a Paint window. You can then edit the image without leaving WordPad, and clicking outside the image will return you to WordPad.

Fig. 7.17 An Embedded Graphic in WordPad.

The **Display As Icon** option in the Insert Object dialogue box (Fig. 7.16), embeds an icon in the destination document. This option is useful for embedding speech or movie clips in a document. Double-clicking the icon would then play the sound, or movie.

Linking a Graphic into WordPad

Linking, the other main OLE feature, links files dynamically so that information held in one file is automatically updated when the information in the other file changes.

To link our graphic to **WordPad**, select the **Link** option in the Insert Object dialogue box of Fig. 7.16, before clicking the **OK** button.

When you double-click a linked image, its file is opened into a separate Paint window. Any changes made are saved in this file as well as being reflected in the document.

OLE (Object Linking and Embedding), is pronounced as 'oh-leh'. It is a compound document standard developed by Microsoft, and incorporated in both the Windows and Macintosh operating systems, which enables you to create objects with one application and then link or embed them in a second application. Embedded objects retain their original format and links to the application that created them.

Controlling Fonts

Windows Vista uses a Font Manager to control the installed fonts on your system. You can use the Font Manager to install new fonts, view examples of existing fonts, and delete fonts. To open the Font Manager, click the **Start** button then click the **Control Panel** menu option to reveal the Control Panel window, part of which is shown (in Classic View) in Fig. 7.18.

Fig. 7.18 The Control Panel Window.

Next, double-click the **Fonts** icon to display the Fonts window, shown in Fig. 7.19.

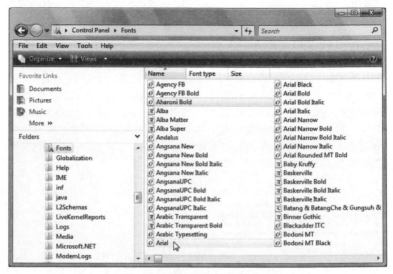

Fig. 7.19 The Fonts Window.

To see an example of one of the listed fonts, double-click its icon in the Fonts window. Below we show the Arial (TrueType) font in four different sizes.

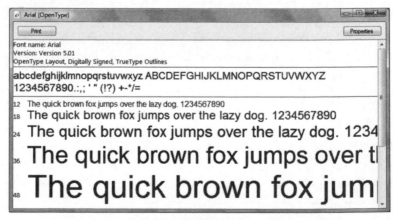

Fig. 7.20 Font Size Sample Window for a Selected Font.

You might find it interesting to know, that the Symbol font contains an abundance of Greek letters, while the Webdings and Wingdings Fonts contain special graphic objects, as shown in Fig. 7.21. Do have a look, you will be amazed!

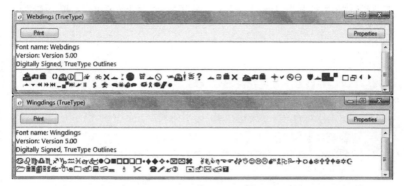

Fig. 7.21 Webdings (top) and Wingdings (bottom) Fonts.

We will explain shortly how such characters can be inserted into a document.

Some Font Basics: Font sizes are measured in 'points' (a point being, approximately 1/72 of an inch), which determine the height of a character. There is another unit of character measurement called the 'pitch' which is the number of characters that can fit horizontally in one inch.

The spacing of a font is either 'fixed' (mono spaced) or 'proportional'. With fixed spacing, each character takes up exactly the same space, while proportionally spaced characters take up different spacing (an 'i' or a 't' take up less space than a 'u' or a 'w'). Thus the length of proportionally spaced text can vary depending on which letters it contains. However, numerals take up the same amount of space whether they have been specified as fixed or proportional.

Windows Vista makes available several 'TrueType' fonts which can be used by Windows applications, such as word processors. TrueType are outline fonts that are rendered from line and curve commands. These types of fonts are scalable to any point size, can be rotated, and look exactly the same on the screen as they do when printed.

Controlling Characters

A useful feature in Windows is the Character Map, shown open in Fig. 7.22. This should be found in the **All Programs, Accessories, System Tools** menu.

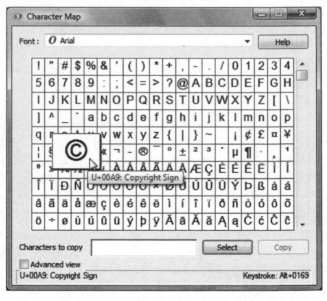

Fig. 7.22 Selecting a Character from the Character Map Utility.

You use this facility from an application, such as a word processor, when you need a special character, such as the 'copyright' sign © shown in Fig. 7.22, to be included in your document.

To copy a special character, not found on your keyboard, into your document, open the **Character Map**, select the **Font**, and click the character to enlarge it, as shown above, click the **Select** button, which places it in the **Characters to copy** box. When you have all the characters you want in this box, clicking the **Copy** button will copy them to the **Clipboard**. Now, return to your application, make sure the insertion point is in the correct position and paste the characters there either with the **Edit**, **Paste** menu command, or the **Ctrl+V** keyboard shortcut.

The Notepad Editor

Notepad is a text editor which can be used to read or write short notes, or create and edit script files. The program, which supports different fonts and their modifications (bold, underline, italic) is usually used to read text files (with the extension **.txt** of less than 64 KB) supplied by different vendors, or to make short text notes. You read such files by double-clicking their filename – trying to read larger files than 64 KB causes **WordPad** to be activated instead (more about this shortly).

To see **Notepad** in operation, we opened the **Memo to PC Users** file in **WordPad**, then saved it as a text file with the **.txt** extension. Then use the **Start**, **All Programs**, **Accessories** command and click the **Notepad** entry. The result is shown in Fig. 7.23 on the next page.

Note that the memo has lost all its enhancements, and the text does not fit in the window chosen, but displays as one long line.

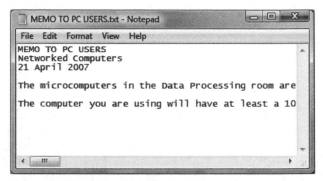

Fig. 7.23 Notepad's Opening Screen.

Notepad's Edit Features

Although **Notepad** is not as powerful as **WordPad**, it has some interesting features, such as the ability to turn on word wrap which causes words that will not fit within its page margins to be placed on the next line automatically. You can turn word wrap on by selecting the **Format**, **Word Wrap** menu command, as shown in Fig. 7.24.

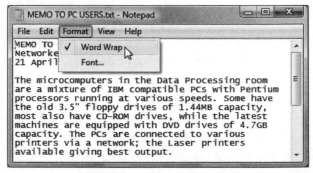

Fig. 7.24 Notepad's Opening Screen.

Another **Notepad** feature is the **Select All** option from the **Edit** menu which allows you to highlight a whole document at a stroke so as to copy it onto the **Clipboard**.

To change the font of a selected text, use the **Format**, **Font** command to display the Font dialogue box shown in Fig. 7.25 below:

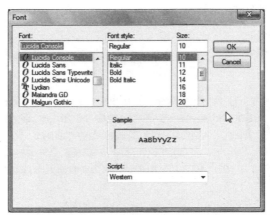

Fig. 7.25 Notepad's Font Dialogue Box.

You can use the Font dialogue box to change the **Font style** and font **Size** of your document. However, any changes you make here are reflected in the whole document, as well as all other documents you open using **Notepad**. In other words, you are configuring **Notepad** to the font, font style and font size you would like to use when reading or writing text files, rather than applying these changes to whole or parts of a document.

Notepad supports the usual edit features, such as cut, copy, paste, and delete, all of which are options of the **Edit** menu. You can even use Notepad to search and find text, by selecting the **Edit**, **Find** command. Once the text is found, pressing the **F3** function key finds the next occurrence. You can also control the **Direction** of the search and use the **Match case** facility.

* * *

In Chapters 8 and 9 we discuss how to connect to the Internet and how to send and receive e-mail using Windows Mail, which is the new name for Outlook Express. Chapter 8 covers the basics, while Chapter 9 delves into e-mail attachments and e-mail organisation.

* * *

8

E-mail – Windows Mail Basics

To be able to communicate electronically with the rest of the world, you will need to connect your computer through some type of modem to an active phone line. A modem is a device that converts data so that it can be transmitted over the telephone system. Making such a connection to the Internet is made very easy with Windows Vista.

To start the process, open the **Welcome Center** which can be found in **Control Panel**, **System and Maintenance** in **Category** view, and click the **Connect to the Internet** option pointed to in Fig. 8.1 below.

Fig. 8.1 The Welcome Center Screen.

This opens the screen in Fig. 8.2, and clicking the **Connect to the Internet** link (pointed to), displays the screen in Fig. 8.3.

Fig. 8.2 Connecting to the Internet Screen.

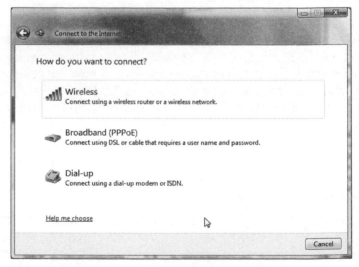

Fig. 8.3 The Three Connection Methods.

As you can see, there are three ways of connecting to the Internet; **Wireless**, **Broadband**, or **Dial-up**.

For a **Wireless** connection you will require a wireless router or a network.

For **Broadband** connection you will need a broadband modem, also called DSL (Digital Subscriber Line), or a cable modem.

For a **Dial-up** connection you will need a modem (most computers come with a 56 Kbps modem already installed), but not a DSL or cable modem.

The choice is yours, but whichever method you select you will need to subscribe to an ISP (Internet Service Provider) and for the first two connection methods you will need to purchase the appropriate hardware.

The Windows Mail

Windows Vista comes with the very powerful mail and news facility, **Windows Mail** (which is really a slightly modified Outlook Express 6), built into it, which makes it very easy for you to send and receive e-mail messages. The program should already have been added to your PC by **Setup** (an entry being placed on the **Start** menu left column. Some users might prefer to have a shortcut to **Windows Mail** on their desktop (right-click it and use the **Send To**, **Desktop** command, while others might prefer to have it placed in the **Quick Launch** area of the **Taskbar** (drag it there). The choice is yours!

To start the program, left-click the menu option on the **Start** menu, shown here, double-click its icon on the desktop, or click its icon on the **Quick Launch** toolbar.

Either of these actions displays the screen below.

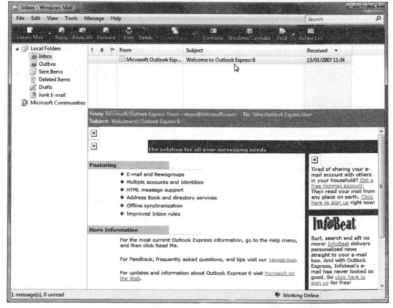

Fig. 8.4 The Windows Mail Opening Screen.

Obviously, to send and receive electronic mail you must be connected to the Internet. There are quite a few providers around, with some providing free Broadband if you subscribe to their telephone package. Once you have registered with such a service, you will be given all the necessary information to connect to the Internet, so that you can fully exploit all its available facilities.

Connecting to your Server

To tell **Windows Mail** how to connect to your server's facilities, you must complete your personal e-mail connection details in the Internet Connection screens, which display when you first attempt to use the **Read Mail** facility pointed to in Fig. 8.5.

If the connection process does not start, or if you want to change your details, use the **Tools**, **Accounts** menu command, as shown below.

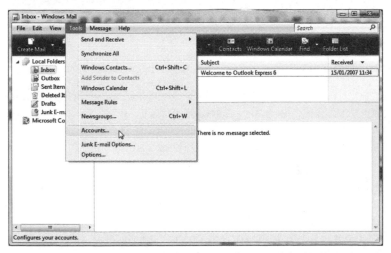

Fig. 8.5 The Internet Accounts Options Screen of Windows Mail.

In the displayed Internet Accounts dialogue box click the **Add** button and in the next screen select **E-mail Account**, and click **Next**.

In the following screen, type your name in the text box, as shown in Fig. 8.6 below.

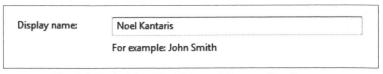

Display name: Noel Kantaris

For example: John Smith

Fig. 8.6 Part of the First Internet Connection Screen.

We only show the relevant parts of the various screens so you know what is expected of you, but remember to type your own details (not what is shown) in these screens, and click the **Next** button to progress from one screen to another.

In the next screen, enter your e-mail address in the text box, as shown in Fig. 8.7 below.

E-mail address:
my-address@my-server.com
For example: someone@microsoft.com

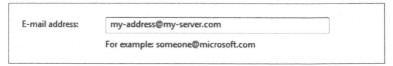

Fig. 8.7 Part of the Second Internet Connection Screen.

If you have not organised one yet you could always sign up for free e-mail with Hotmail, which is a free browser-based e-mail service owned by Microsoft – we will discuss this in Chapter 10 (page 206).

In the third connection screen enter your e-mail server details, as shown for us in Fig. 8.8 below. To complete some of the details here you may need to ask your Internet Service Provider (ISP), or system administrator, for help. The details shown below will obviously only work for the writer, so please don't try them!

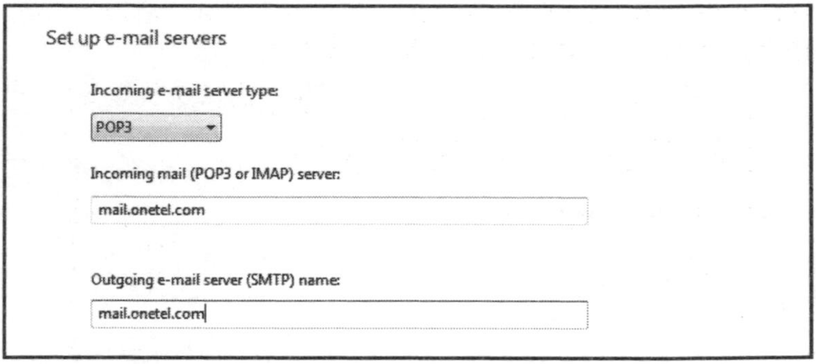

Set up e-mail servers
Incoming e-mail server type:
POP3
Incoming mail (POP3 or IMAP) server:
mail.onetel.com
Outgoing e-mail server (SMTP) name:
mail.onetel.com

Fig. 8.8 Part of the Third Internet Connection Screen.

The next screen asks for your user name and password. Both these would have been given to you by your ISP. Type these in, as shown in Fig. 8.9 on the next page. Obviously the password you were given by your ISP, consists of letters and numbers, but as you type these in, they display as asterisks.

If you select the **Remember password** option in this box, you will not have to enter these details every time you log on. **BUT** it may not be wise to do this if your PC is in a busy office – for security reasons.

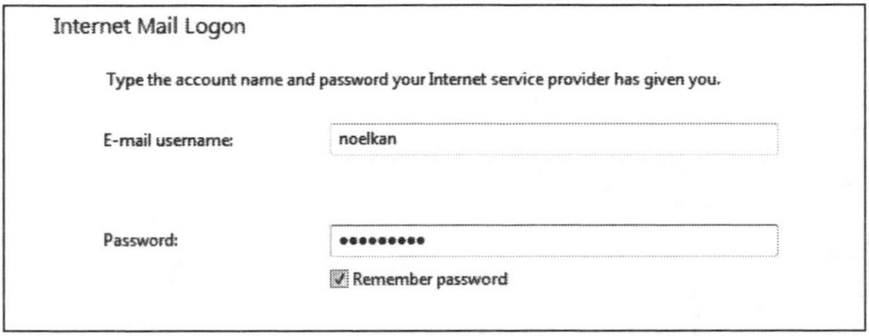

Internet Mail Logon

Type the account name and password your Internet service provider has given you.

E-mail username: noelkan

Password: •••••••••

☑ Remember password

Fig. 8.9 Part of the Fourth Internet Connection Screen.

Pressing **Next**, leads to the final connection screen informing you of your success, which completes the procedure, so click **Finish** to return to the Internet Accounts tabbed window, with your new mail account set up as shown for us in Fig. 8.10 below.

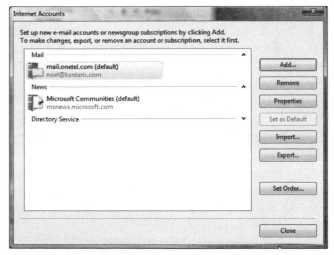

Fig. 8.10 The Internet Mail Accounts Window.

Once your connection is established, you can click the **Read Mail** coloured link, or the **Inbox** entry in the **Folder List** to read your mail. Opening the **Inbox** for the first time, will probably display a message from Microsoft, like that shown in Fig. 8.11.

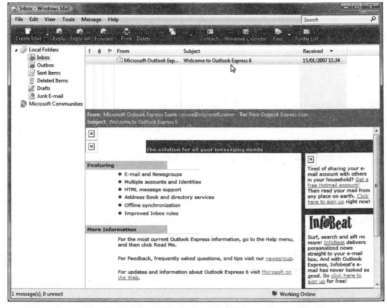

Fig. 8.11 The Windows Mail Inbox Screen.

This shows the default Windows Mail main screen layout, which consists of a **Folders List** to the left, a set of toolbar buttons, including the new **Contacts** and **Windows Calendar** buttons, a **Message List** to the top right of the screen, and a **Preview** pane below that. The list under **Folders** contains all the active mail folders, news servers and newsgroups. Clicking on one of these displays its contents in the **Message List**. Clicking on a message opens a preview of it, while double-clicking on a message opens the message in its own window.

Receiving an E-mail

To check your mail, click the **Send/Recv** toolbar icon which, if you are using a Dial-up connection will display the Dial-up Connection window, but if you are on 'always on' Broadband it will automatically download your messages.

With a dial-up connection you will have to click the **Connect** button on the displayed dialogue box to activate your modem and connect you to the Internet. If you have any new messages, they will then be downloaded from your mailbox to your hard disc.

Double-clicking on the connection image on the extreme right of the **Taskbar**, shown here, displays your connection **Status** window. The exact display depends on the type of connection, but you can use it to disconnect your computer from the Internet. This is only advisable if you are on Dial-up, because disconnecting your PC from the Internet allows you to read and process your mail at your leisure without still paying for a telephone connection. On Broadband this is not relevant.

Sending a Test E-mail Message

Before explaining in more detail the main features of **Windows Mail** we will step through the procedure of sending a very simple e-mail message. The best way to test out any unfamiliar e-mail features is to send a test message to your own e-mail address. This saves wasting somebody else's time, and the message can be very quickly checked to see the results.

To start, click the **Create Mail** icon to open the New Message window, shown in Fig. 8.12 on the next page.

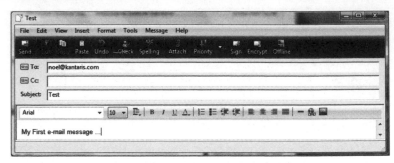

Fig. 8.12 Creating a New E-mail.

Type your own e-mail address in the **To:** field, and a title for the message in the **Subject:** field. The text in this subject field will form a header for the message when it is received, so it helps to show in a few words what the message is about. Type your message and click the **Send** toolbar icon shown here.

By default, your message is stored in an **Outbox** folder and, if you are on 'always on' Broadband it will be sent immediately, otherwise you will have to press the **Send/Recv** toolbar icon to connect to the Internet so it can be sent, hopefully straight into your mailbox.

When **Windows Mail** next checks for mail, it will find the message and download it into the **Inbox** folder, for you to read.

The Main Windows Mail Screen

After the initial opening window, **Windows Mail** uses three other main windows, which we will refer to as: the Main screen which opens next; the Read Message screen for reading your mail; and the New Message screen, to compose your outgoing mail messages.

The Main screen consists of a toolbar, a menu, and four panes with the default display shown in our example in Fig. 8.11. You can choose different pane layouts, and customise the toolbar, with the **View**, **Layout** menu command, but we will let you try these for yourself.

The Folders List

The **Folders** pane contains a list of your mail folders, your news servers and any newsgroups you have subscribed to. There are always at least six mail folders, as shown in Fig. 8.13 below. You can add your own with the **File**, **Folder**, **New** menu command from the Main window. You can delete added folders with the **File**, **Folder**, **Delete** command. These operations can also be carried out after right-clicking a folder in the list. You can drag messages from the **Message** list and drop them into any of the folders, to 'store' them there.

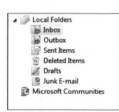

Fig. 8.13 The Local Folders Pane.

Note the icons shown in Fig. 8.13; any new folders you add will have the same icon as that of the first added folder.

The Message List

When you select a folder, by clicking it in the **Folders** list, the **Message** list shows the contents of that folder. Brief details of each message are displayed on one line, as shown in Fig. 8.14 below.

!	θ	ℙ	From	Subject	Received ▾
			⊠ Noel Kantaris	Test	27/02/2007 17:03
			⊠ Microsoft Outlook Exp...	Welcome to Outlook Express 6	15/01/2007 11:34

Fig. 8.14 Received Messages in Descending Date Order.

The first column shows the message priority, if any, the second whether the message has an attachment, and the third whether the message has been 'flagged'. All of these are indicated by icons on the message line.

The 'From' column shows the message status icon (see Fig. 8.16) and the name of the sender, 'Subject' shows the title of each mail message, and 'Received' shows the date it reached you. You can control what columns display in this pane with the **View**, **Columns** menu command.

To sort a list of messages, you can click the mouse pointer in the title of the column you want the list sorted on, clicking it again will sort it in reverse order. The sorted column is shown with a triangle mark, as shown in Fig. 8.15 below.

Fig. 8.15 Received Messages in Ascending Date Order.

This shows the received messages sorted by date, with the most recently received message appearing at the top. This is our preferred method of display.

The Preview Pane

When you select a message in the **Message** list, by clicking it once, it is displayed in the **Preview** pane, which takes up the rest of the window. This lets you read the first few lines to see if the message is worth bothering with. If so, double-clicking the header, in the **Message** list, will open the message in the Read Message window, as shown later in the chapter. You could use the **Preview** pane to read all your mail, especially if your messages are all on the short side, but it is easier to process them from the Read Message window.

Message Status Icons

This icon	Indicates this
📎	The message has one or more files attached.
!	The message has been marked high priority by the sender.
↓	The message has been marked low priority by the sender.
📖	The message has been read. The message heading appears in light type.
✉	The message has not been read. The message heading appears in bold type.
🗨	The message has been replied to.
🗨	The message has been forwarded.
🗐	The message is in progress in the Drafts folder.
🖃	The message is digitally signed and unopened.
🖃	The message is encrypted and unopened.
🖃	The message is digitally signed, encrypted and unopened.
🖂	The message is digitally signed and has been opened.
🖂	The message is encrypted and has been opened.
🖂	The message is digitally signed and encrypted, and has been opened.
⊞	The message has responses that are collapsed. Click the icon to show all the responses (expand the conversation).
⊟	The message and all of its responses are expanded. Click the icon to hide all the responses (collapse the conversation).
▽	The unread message header is on an IMAP server.
✗	The opened message is marked for deletion on an IMAP server.
⚑	The message is flagged.
↓	The IMAP message is marked to be downloaded.
⊞↓	The IMAP message and all conversations are marked to be downloaded.
⊟↓	The individual IMAP message (without conversations) is marked to be downloaded.

Fig. 8.16. Table of Message Status Icons.

Note: If you have used Outlook Express before on Windows XP, you will be wondering what has happen to the **Contacts** pane. The answer is 'not available in Windows Mail', but there is a way around this, if you want to have your contacts on the desktop, as follows:

Click the + sign on the **Gadgets** pane on the desktop, and select **Contacts** from the displayed Gadgets screen. We will explain how to use it in Chapter 9 (page 184).

The Main Window Toolbar

Selecting any one of the local folders displays the following buttons on Outlook's toolbar.

 Opens the New Message window for creating a new mail message, with the **To:** field blank.

 Opens the New Message window for replying to the current mail message, with the **To:** field pre-addressed to the original sender. The original **Subject** field is prefixed with **Re:**.

 Opens the New Message window for replying to the current mail message, with the **To:** field pre-addressed to all that received copies of the original message. The original **Subject** field is prefixed with **Re:**.

 Opens the New Message window for forwarding the current mail message. The **To:** field is blank. The original **Subject** field is prefixed with **Fw:**.

 Prints the selected message.

 Deletes the currently selected message and places it in the **Deleted Items** folder.

 Connects to the mailbox server and downloads waiting messages, which it places in the **Inbox** folder. Sends any messages waiting in the **Outbox** folder.

 Opens the **Contacts** list.

 Opens the **Windows Calendar**.

Finds a message or an e-mail address using the **Find People** facility of the **Contacts** list.

 Toggles the **Folders** list on or off.

The Read Message Window

If you double-click a message in the **Message** list of the Main window, the Read Message window is opened as shown in Fig. 8.17 below.

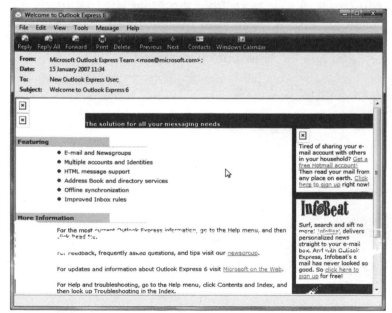

Fig. 8.17 The Read Message Window.

This is the best window to read your mail in. It has its own menu system and toolbar, which lets you rapidly process and move between the messages in a folder.

The Read Message Toolbar

This window has its own toolbar, but only two icons are different from those in the Main window.

Previous – Displays the previous mail message in the Read Message window.

Next – Displays the next mail message in the Read Message window.

These buttons give an audible warning if there are no previous or further messages.

Signing your E-mail

You create a signature from the Main window using the **Tools**, **Options** command which opens the Options dialogue box shown in Fig. 8.18 when its Signature tab is selected and the **New** button is clicked.

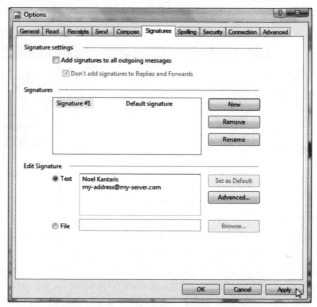

Fig. 8.18 The Tools Options Window.

You could choose to add your signature to all outgoing messages which is preferable, but click the **Advanced** button and check which account you would like this signature to apply to, or use the **Insert**, **Signature** command from the **New Message** window menu system.

The New Message Window

This is the window, shown in Fig. 8.19, that you will use to create any messages you want to send electronically from Outlook Express. It is important to understand its features, so that you can get the most out of it.

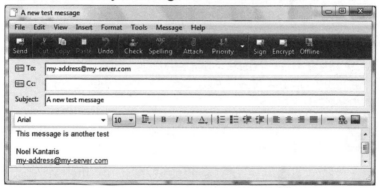

Fig. 8.19 The New Message Window.

As we saw, this window can be opened by using the **Create Mail** toolbar icon from the Main window, as well as the **Message**, **New Message** menu command. From other windows you can also use the **Message**, **New Message** command, or the **Ctrl+N** keyboard shortcut. The newly opened window has its own menu system and toolbar, which let you rapidly prepare (you don't need to be connected to the Internet for that), and send your new e-mail messages after connecting to the Internet. If you are on Broadband, of course, you might always be connected to the Internet.

Using Message Stationery

Another **Windows Mail** feature is that it lets you send your messages on pre-formatted stationery for added effect.

To access these, click the down arrow next to the **Create Mail** button in the Main window and either select from the **1** to **10** list, as shown here, or use the **Select Stationery** command to preview them.

Fig. 8.20 Using Stationery.

The New Message Toolbar

The icons on the New Message toolbar window have the following functions:

Send – Sends message, either to the recipient, or to the **Outbox** folder.

Cut – Cuts selected text to the Windows **Clipboard**.

Copy – Copies selected text to the Windows **Clipboard**.

Paste – Pastes the contents of the Windows **Clipboard** into the current message.

Undo – Undoes the last editing action.

Check – Checks that names match your entries in the **Contacts** list, or are in correct e-mail address format.

Spelling – Checks the spelling of the current message before it is sent, but is only available if you have **Word**, **Excel**, or **PowerPoint**.

Attach – Opens the Insert Attachment window for you to select a file to be attached to the current message.

Priority – Sets the message priority as high or low, to indicate its importance to the recipient.

Sign – Adds a digital signature to the message to confirm to the recipient that it is from you.

Encrypt – Encodes the message so that only the recipient can read it.

Offline – Closes connection to the Internet so that you can process your mail offline. The button then changes to **Work Online.**

Message Formatting

Windows Mail provides quite sophisticated formatting options for an e-mail editor from both the **Format** menu

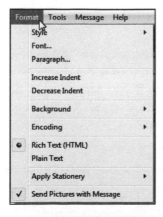

and toolbar. These only work if you prepare the message in HTML format, as used in Web documents. You can set this to be your default mail sending format using the Send tab in the **Tools**, **Options** box of the Read Message window (see Fig. 8.17).

Fig. 8.21 The Format Sub-menu.

To use the format for the current message only, select **Rich Text (HTML)** from the **Format** menu, as we have done in Fig. 8.21. If **Plain Text** is selected, the blue dot will be placed against this option on the menu, and the formatting features will not then be available.

The **Format** toolbar shown in Fig. 8.22 below is added to the New Message window when you are in HTML mode and all the **Format** menu options are then made active.

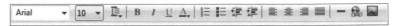

Fig. 8.22 The Format Toolbar.

As all the formatting features are self-explanatory, we will not delve into them here – most of these are quite well demonstrated in Microsoft's opening message to you. You should be able to prepare some very easily readable e-mail messages with these features, but remember that not everyone will be able to read the work in the way that you spent hours creating. Only e-mail programs that support MIME (Multipurpose Internet Mail Extensions) can read HTML formatting. When your recipient's e-mail program does not read HTML, and many people choose not to, the message appears as plain text with an HTML file attached.

Note: At the risk of being called boring we think it is usually better to stick to plain text without the selection of any message stationery, particularly if you are using a 56 Kbps modem; not only can everyone read it, but it is much quicker to transmit and deal with.

Replying to a Message

When you receive an e-mail message that you want to reply to, Windows Mail makes it very easy to do. The reply address and the new message subject fields are both added automatically for you. Also, by default, the original message is quoted in the reply window for you to edit as required.

With the message you want to reply to still open, click the **Reply** toolbar icon to open the New Message window and the message you are replying to will, by default, be placed under the insertion point.

With long messages, you should not leave all of the original text in your reply. This can be bad practice, which rapidly makes new messages very large and time consuming to download. You should usually edit the quoted text, so that it is obvious what you are referring to. A few lines may be enough.

Removing Deleted Messages

Whenever you delete a message it is actually moved to the **Deleted Items** folder. If ignored, this folder gets bigger and bigger over time, so you need to check it frequently and manually re-delete messages you are sure you will not need again.

Alternatively, use the **Tools**, **Options** menu command on the Read Message window to open the Options dialogue box, click the Advance tab and click the **Maintenance** button at the bottom of the screen. Next, check the **Empty messages from the 'Deleted Items' folder on exit** box in the displayed Maintenance screen, as shown in Fig. 8.23 on the next page.

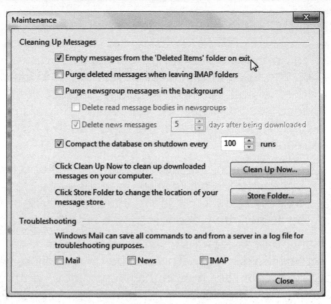

Fig. 8.23 Cleaning up Messages.

* * *

In the next chapter we discuss how to send a picture or a word processed document as an attachment to an e-mail, how to organise your e-mail folders and how to print an e-mail.

* * *

9

E-mail – Some Other Features

Using E-mail Attachments

If you want to include an attachment with your main e-mail message, you simply click the **Attach** toolbar button in the New Message window, as shown in Fig. 9.1.

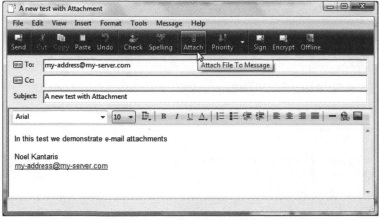

Fig. 9.1 Adding an Attachment to an E-mail.

This opens the Insert Attachment dialogue box, shown in Fig. 9.2 on the next page, for you to select the file, or files, you want to go with your message.

If, however, you are attaching pictures whose size is larger than 100 KB, then please refer to the method described at the end of Chapter 4 (page 78), on how to reduce their size automatically before attaching them to your e-mail.

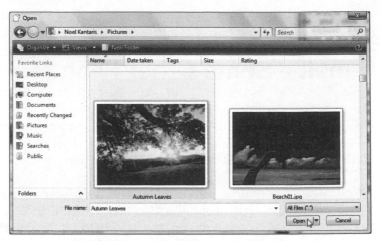

Fig. 9.2 The Insert Attachment Dialogue Box.

In **Windows Mail** the attached files are placed below the **Subject** text box. In Fig. 9.3 we show two attachments with their distinctive icons that tell the recipient what each file is; a graphics (**.jpg**) file and a Word (**.doc**) document in this case.

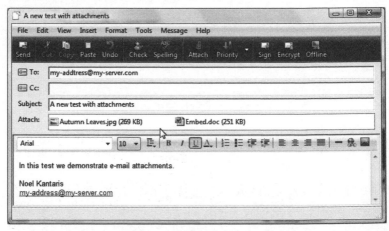

Fig. 9.3 Adding an Attachment to an E-mail.

It is only polite to include in your e-mail a short description of what the attachments are, and which applications were used to create them; it will help the recipient to decipher them.

Clicking the **Send** icon on the toolbar, puts each e-mail (with its attachments, if any) in Mail's **Outbox** folder. Next time you click the **Send/Recv** toolbar icon, Windows Mail connects to your ISP and sends all the e-mail messages stored in it.

Sending an E-mail to the Drafts Folder

If you decide that your e-mail is not complete yet and further changes are needed before sending it, use the **File**, **Send Later** command, as shown in Fig. 9.4 below.

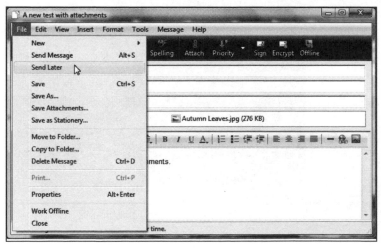

Fig. 9.4 Send an E-mail Later.

This displays a message telling you that the e-mail will be placed in the **Outbox** and will not be sent until the next time you click the **Send/Recv** button. You should now locate this e-mail in the **Outbox** and drag it into the **Drafts** folder for safe keeping until you need to change it.

To edit an e-mail waiting in the **Drafts** folder, click the folder, then double-click the e-mail to open it in its own window, edit it, and click the **Send** icon on the toolbar.

Receiving Attachments with an E-mail

To demonstrate what happens when you receive an e-mail with attachments, we have sent the above e-mail to our ISP, then a minute or so later we received it back, as shown in Fig. 9.5 below.

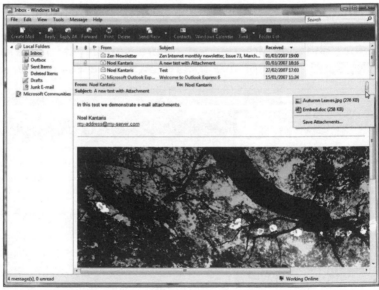

Fig. 9.5 A Received E-mail with Attachments.

Note that the received e-mail shows the graphics (**.jpg**) file open at the bottom of the **Preview** pane, but there is no indication of any other attachments. To find out how many attachments were included with the received e-mail, left-click the **Attach** (paper clip) icon pointed to in Fig. 9.5 to display all of them, as shown above in the drop-down menu.

Left-clicking the graphics attachment file (**.jpg**) opens it in **Windows Photo Gallery**, while left-clicking the document file opens the Mail Attachment screen shown here in Fig. 9.6.

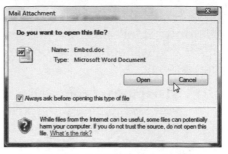

Fig. 9.6 The Mail Attachment Box.

Each document file can be opened in situ or saved later to disc from within the application that opened it.

Organising your Messages

Probably most of the e-mail messages you get you will delete once you have dealt with them. Some however you may well need to keep for future reference. After a few weeks it can be surprising how many of these messages can accumulate. If you don't do something with them they seem to take over and slow the whole process down. That is the reason for the **Folders List**.

As we saw earlier you can open folders in this area, and can move and copy messages from one folder into another. You can move messages by highlighting their header line in the **Message List** and dragging them into another folder. The copy procedure is the same, except you must also have the **Ctrl** key depressed through the dragging procedure. You can tell that copying is taking place by the '+' on the mouse pointer as shown here to the right.

Fig. 9.7 Moving a Message.

The System Folders

Windows Mail has six folders which it always keeps intact and will not let you delete. Some of these we have met already.

- The **Inbox** folder holds all incoming messages; you should delete or move them from this folder as soon as you have read them. Messages in the **Inbox** folder can be moved or copied into any other folder except the **Outbox** folder.

- The **Outbox** folder holds messages that have been prepared but not yet transmitted. As soon as the messages are sent they are automatically removed to the **Sent Items** folder. Messages in the **Outbox** folder can be moved or copied into any of the other folders.

- The **Sent Items** folder holds messages that have been transmitted. You can then decide whether to 'file' your copies of these messages, or whether to delete them. Messages in the **Sent Items** folder can be moved or copied into any of the other folders except the **Outbox** folder.

- The **Deleted Items** folder holds messages that have been deleted and placed in there as a safety feature. Messages in the **Deleted Items** folder can be moved or copied into any of the other folders, except the **Outbox** folder.

- The **Drafts** folder is used to hold a message you closed down without sending by selecting the **File**, **Send Later** menu command, then dragged it from the **Outbox** folder where it was saved into the **Drafts** folder. Messages in the **Draft** folder cannot be moved or copied into any of the other folders. Simply double-click such a message to open it in its own window, edit it, and click the **Send** button.

- The **Junk E-mail** folder is designed to catch unsolicited e-mail messages, called 'spam'. You can increase or decrease the junk e-mail protection level by clicking **Tools**, **Junk E-mail Options** and select the level of protection.

To create additional folders, highlight the folder under which you want to create a sub-folder – here we have chosen to create a sub-folder under **Local Folders**. Right-clicking the selected folder and choosing the **New Folder** option from the drop-down menu, as shown in Fig. 9.8, displays the Create Folder dialogue box shown in Fig. 9.9 below.

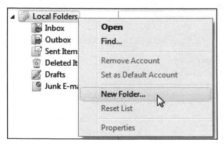

Fig. 9.8 Creating a New Folder.

Next, type an appropriate name for the new folder and click the **OK** button to add the newly created folder to the **Local Folders** list.

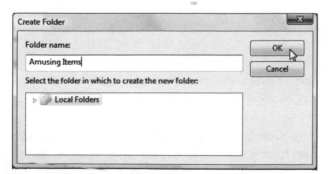

Fig. 9.9 The New Folder Dialogue Box.

Using Message Rules

If you have a problem with junk mail, use the **Message Rules** menu option to filter your incoming messages. Unwanted ones can be placed in your **Deleted Items** folder straight away. It can also be useful for sorting incoming messages and automatically directing them to their correct folders. To open this feature (Fig. 9.10), use the **Tools**, **Message Rules**, **Mail** menu command.

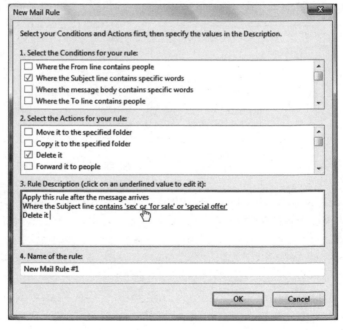

Fig. 9.10 Creating Message Rules, Box 1.

In the Section 1 of Fig. 9.10, you select the conditions for the new rule. In Section 2 you control what actions are taken, and the new rule itself is automatically 'built' for you in Section 3. If you use this feature much, you will probably want to name each of your rules in Section 4.

In Fig. 9.11 below, we have set to intercept and delete messages which contain certain words in their Subject Lines. To complete the rule we clicked on the 'contains specific words' link in Fig. 9.10 and filled in the following dialogue box, clicking the **Add** button after each phrase.

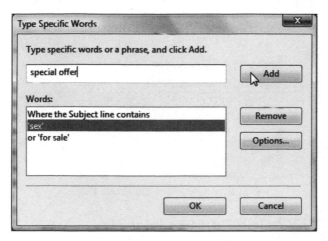

Fig. 9.11 Entering Words to Act Upon.

When finished clicking on **OK** twice opens the Message Rules dialogue box shown in Fig. 9.12 on the next page. In this box you can control your rules. You can set multiple rules for incoming messages and control the sort priority for the list. The higher up a multiple list a condition is the higher will be its priority.

If an incoming message matches more than one rule, then it is sorted according to the first rule it matches in your list.

The **Message, Create Rule from Message** menu command is a quick way to start the **New Mail Rule** process, as the details of the currently selected message are automatically placed in the New Mail Rule dialogue box for you.

Fig. 9.12 The Message Rules Box.

The Blocked Senders List

With **Windows Mail** there is a very easy way to prevent messages from a problem source ever disturbing your peace again. When you first receive a problem message, select it in the **Messages List** and action the **Message**, **Junk E-mail**, **Add Sender to Block Senders List** menu command, as we did in the example in Fig. 9.13 below.

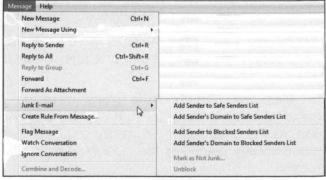

Fig. 9.13 Blocking Messages from a Single Source.

This can be a very powerful tool, but be careful how you use it. If you are not careful, you may block messages that you really would rather have received!

Spell Checking your Messages

Just because e-mail messages are a quick way of getting in touch with friends and family, there is no reason why they should be full of spelling mistakes. Some people do not seem to read their work before clicking the **Send** button. With Windows Mail this should be a thing of the past, as the program is linked to the spell checker that comes with other Microsoft programs. If you do not have any of these, the option will be greyed out, meaning that it is not available.

To try it out, prepare a message in the New Message window, but make an obvious spelling mistake, maybe like ours below. Pressing the **Spelling** toolbar button, or using the **Tools, Spelling** menu command, reveals the drop-down sub-menu shown in Fig. 9.14 below.

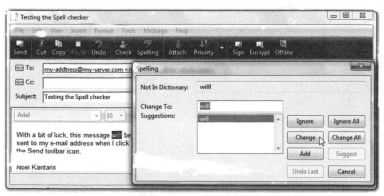

Fig. 9.14 Using the Spell Checker.

Any words not recognised by the spell checker will be flagged up as shown. If you are happy with the word just click one of the **Ignore** buttons, if not, you can type a correction in the **Change To:** field, or accept one of the **Suggestions:**, and then click the **Change** button.

You can get some control over the spell checker on the settings sheet opened from the main **Windows Mail** menu with the **Tools**, **Options** command, and then clicking the Spelling tab.

The available options, as shown in Fig. 9.15, are self-explanatory so we will not dwell on them. If you want every message to be checked before it is sent, select the **Always check spelling before sending** option.

Fig. 9.15 The Options Spelling Dialogue Box.

You could also choose to have the Spell Checker ignore **Words with numbers**, before clicking the **Apply** button.

Printing your Messages

Windows Mail lets you print e-mail messages to paper, but it does not give you any control over the page settings it uses. You can, however, alter the font size of your printed output as it depends on the font size you set for viewing your messages. As shown here, you have five 'relative' size options available from the **View**, **Text Size** menu command.

Fig. 9.16 The View Menu.

When you are ready to print a message in the Read Message window, use the **Ctrl+P** key combination, or the **File**, **Print** menu command, to open the Print dialogue box shown in Fig. 9.17 with its General tab selected.

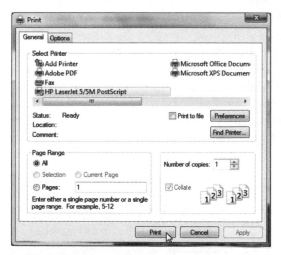

Fig. 9.17 The Print Dialogue Box.

Make sure the correct printer, **Page Range**, and **Number of copies** you want are selected, then click **Print**. You can also start the printing procedure by clicking the **Print** toolbar icon shown here.

If the message has Web page links on it, there are two useful features in the Options tab of the Print dialogue box shown in Fig. 9.17. These are:

- The **Print all linked documents** option, which when checked not only prints the message, but also all the Web pages linked to it.

- The **Print table of links** option, which when checked, gives a hard copy listing of the URL addresses of all the links present in the page.

The Windows Contacts Utility

The **Windows Contacts** utility can be used not only with the E-mail application, but also with the Fax utility (discussed earlier in Chapter 5, page 90). Fax numbers are, of course, straightforward to deal with, but e-mail addresses are often quite complicated and not at all easy to remember. Windows provides a **Contacts** utility in which Fax numbers, telephone numbers, and e-mail addresses can be gathered together and used by its various communication applications.

To access the **Contacts** utility, use the **Start**, **All Programs**, **Windows Contacts** menu command. In Fig. 9.18 we show part of an example. Once in **Windows Contacts**, you can manually add a person's details, Fax number and e-mail address in the Properties dialogue box.

Fig. 9.18 The Windows Contacts Screen.

You can open the Properties dialogue box by clicking the **New Contact** icon in Fig. 9.18 above to display the screen shown in Fig. 9.19 below.

Fig. 9.19 The Windows Contacts Screen.

Use the Name and E-mail tab to enter the name, title, and e-mail address for the recipient. The Home tab screen is used to enter the recipient's address, telephone, Fax number, and Web site. You can also enter similar information for Work. The rest of the information pertaining to an individual can be entered later as it is needed, by editing a Contact's entry.

Selecting **New Contact Group** from the Contacts screen of Fig. 9.18, lets you create a grouping of e-mail addresses, you can then send mail to everyone in the group with one operation.

To send a new message to anyone listed in your **Contacts** list, open the **Windows Mail** application, click the **Create Mail** toolbar icon to open the New Message window, and use the **Tools**, **Select Recipients** command, or click on any of the **To:** or **Cc:** icons shown here on the left.

In the Select Recipients dialogue box which is shown

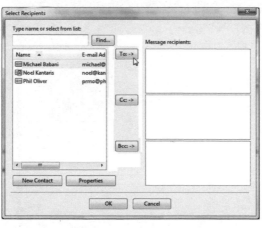

Fig. 9.20 The Select Recipients Screen.

open in Fig. 9.20, you can select a person's name and click either the **To:** button to place it in the **To:** field of your message, the **Cc:** button to place it in the **Cc:** field, or the **Bcc:** button to place it in the **Bcc:** field.

Deleting Individual Contacts

Windows Contacts is highly unstable when it comes to deleting an individual from the **Contacts** list. For example, selecting a person on the **Contacts** list and pressing the **Delete** key on the keyboard stops the program. The same thing happens if you right-click a selected entry and select the **Delete** menu option.

The only way we have found to remove an individual from the **Contacts** list is to open the **Windows Mail** and

click the down arrow against the **Find** toolbar icon shown here, then click the **People** entry from the drop-down menu.

Next, type the name of the person you want to remove from your **Contacts** list in the displayed Find People dialogue box and click the **Find Now** button which opens the bottom half of the screen shown in Fig. 9.21 below.

Fig. 9.21 The Find People Screen.

Clicking the **Delete** button pointed to in the screen above, removes the selected person from the list.

Windows Mail Help

Windows Mail has a built-in Help system, which is accessed with the **Help**, **View Help** menu command, or the **F1** function key. Either of these opens a Help window, as shown in Fig. 9.22 below.

We strongly recommend that you work your way through most the items listed in this window. Clicking on a link opens a separate window with information on the selected topic.

* * *

In the next Chapter we introduce the Internet Explorer 7 which was released a few months prior to the release of Windows Vista.

* * *

Fig. 9.22 The Windows Mail Help System.

10

Using the Internet Explorer

To start the **Internet Explorer**, either click **Start**, **All Programs**, and select **Internet Explorer** from the cascade menu, or click its icon 🏉 on the **Quick Launch** area of the **Taskbar** to the right of the **Start** button (if you can't see these icons, right-click an empty part of the **Taskbar** and select **Toolbars**, **Quick Launch** from the displayed menu). Clicking either of these options opens the Internet browser. The first time you do this, and if you haven't already carried out the procedure of connecting to the Internet described in Chapter 8, you will probably be stepped through the process of establishing a connection to the Internet, as shown in Fig. 10.1.

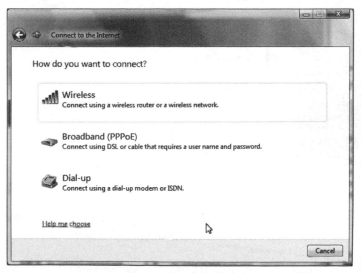

Fig. 10.1 The New Connection Screen.

This procedure can make the process of setting up your Internet connection quite painless. You can open it at any time by clicking the **Tools** toolbar icon, selecting **Internet Options** from the drop-down menu and clicking the **Setup** button on the Connections tabbed sheet. Before starting this operation be sure to find out from your Internet Service Provider (ISP), exactly what settings you will need to enter – please refer to Chapter 8 (page 152).

To get your first look at the **Internet Explorer**, start it as explained on the previous page and log on to the Internet. You may get an opening screen similar to that in Fig. 10.2, but what actually appears will depend on Microsoft, your Internet Service Provider (ISP), or your choice (see next page).

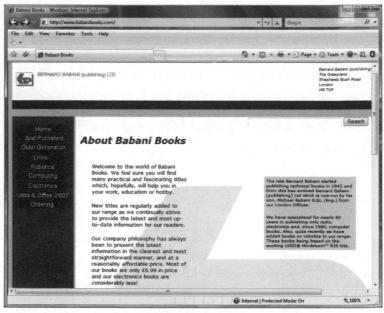

Fig. 10.2 A Typical First Opening Screen.

Note that when the **Explorer** is actually downloading data from the network, the Indicator on the active tab at the top left of the explorer screen (to the right of the two asterisks), and shown here, gives a brief indication of what is actually happening – Connecting... in this case, with a rotating multicoloured circle in front of it.

You can control what Web page is displayed when you start **Explorer** (called your home page), in the **General** settings sheet opened with the **Tools**, **Internet Options** menu command. Select **Use Current** to make any currently open page your home page, or **Use Blank** to show a clear window whenever you start **Explorer**. The **Use Default** option opens the Microsoft Web site **ukmsm.com**.

Your PC Settings

Before we go any further, a few words on screen display resolutions may be useful. Your computer may well have started life set to a screen resolution of 800 x 600 pixels. It then displays a screen of 800 pixels wide and 600 pixels high on the monitor. The bigger the monitor you have, the bigger the screen resolution you can use, as everything gets smaller as the resolution goes up.

For Web browsing you want as large a resolution as you can get so that you can fit more on the screen. Web pages are almost always too large to fit on one screen. We recommend using a resolution of 1280 x 800 (or higher) for 14", 15.4" and larger monitors. For a 14" monitor you might have to change the size of the font in order to read what is on the screen comfortably. We have already discussed how to change the screen settings in Chapter 5. In particular, refer to page 85 on how to change the font size of the displayed text.

Searching the Web

There are many millions of Web pages to look at on the Web, so where do we start? You may have started already from the opening page, but there is one UK institution that we all know, and don't particularly love; 'DVLA' the Driver and Vehicle Licensing Agency. There is a lot of information on their Web site, so let's take a quick look.

 Start **Explorer**, if it is not already going, log onto the Internet, then type dvla in the Search box and click the **Search** button, as shown here. This opens an Explorer screen which should be similar to the one shown in Fig. 10.3. In our case, this displayed several links to pages on the DVLA site. Clicking the **Driver and Vehicle Licensing Agency** link in Fig. 10.3, opens a screen similar to the one shown in Fig. 10.4 on the next page.

Fig. 10.3 The Search Bar.

Fig. 10.4 Using the Search Bar.

From here you can choose links (shown as blue underlined text) or a menu option that might be of interest to you. Do bear in mind that this and subsequent screens of this Web site might be different by the time you access them. Moving the mouse over such links, menu options or even some graphics, changes the pointer to a hand 🖑. Clicking the modified pointer, takes you to different parts of the Web site where you can get information on various topics. That's the beauty of the Internet, once you find your way around you can get almost any up-to-date information you need without moving from your desk.

Explorer can use various search engines so your search may not use the *Live Search* facility which is, in fact, the Microsoft default service using the *msn Search* 'engine'. The *msn Search* utility is just one of many search engines available for finding your way round the Web. A very good search engine we like to use, is Google (www.google.com) in which you can choose to only download pages from UK sites. Hopefully the results from such search engines will be similar.

The Address Bar

If we had known the URL (Uniform Resource Locator) address of the site we wanted, **www.dvla.gov.uk** in our case, we could have typed it straight into the **Internet Explorer Address** bar, as shown below.

Fig. 10.5 Using the Address Bar.

This will open the Web page shown in Fig. 10.4 when the **Enter** key on the keyboard is pressed, or the ➡ (**Go**) button on the right of the address bar is clicked.

The **Address** bar is the main way of opening new Web pages that replace the displayed Web page. A pull-down menu, opened by clicking the down-arrow at the right of the address box, lets you choose from the most recent locations you have typed here, as shown in Fig. 10.6, which can save both effort and errors.

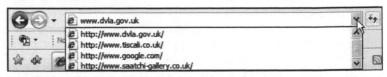

Fig. 10.6 The Pull-down Menu of the Address Bar.

Note that the **Go** button has changed to a ⟳ (**Refresh**) button which when clicked, reloads the Web page shown in the **Address** bar.

The status bar, at the bottom of the screen (Fig. 10.7), shows the URL address of the link pointed to and the loading progress of the Web page in question.

Fig. 10.7 The Pull-down Menu of the Address Bar.

The Explorer Toolbars

As we have discussed earlier in this book, Windows applications are now fully equipped with toolbar options, and **Internet Explorer** is no exception. They contain a series of buttons that you can click with your mouse pointer to quickly carry out a program function.

Fig. 10.8 The Explorer Toolbar.

Most of the buttons are pretty self-explanatory and have the following functions:

Button	*Function*
Back	Displays the previous page viewed, or selects from the drop-down **History** list.
Forward	Displays the next page on the **History** list.
Refresh	Brings a fresh copy of the current Web page to the viewer.
Stop	Halts any on-line transfer of page data.
Search	Searches for the text typed into the **Search** box.
Favorites	Opens the **Favorites Center** from which you can choose the **Favorites**, **Feeds** or **History** bars.
Add to	Adds a favourite site to the **Favorites** bar.
Quick Tabs	Displays all the sites currently loaded into the **Explorer** in one window.

New Tab	Allows you to load another Web site into the current Explorer window. More about this shortly.
Home	Displays your specified home page, with a Microsoft page as the default.
Feeds	Updates Web sites content. It is usually used for news and blogs (Web logs) on Web sites. If a feed is detected the colour of the icon changes from grey to orange.
Print	Prints the open Web page, or frame, using the current print settings.
Page	Allows you to save a current page, send the page or a link to the page by e-mail to a recipient.
Tools	Displays a drop-down menu that allows you, amongst several options, to delete the browsing **History**, manage pop-ups, set 'phishing' filters, and specify your Internet options.
Help	Gives quick access to **Help** topics.
Research	Allows you to carry out research into a specific subject.
Messenger	Gives you access to 'Chat Rooms', or starts a Wizard for you to join the Windows **.net Messenger** service.

You can display additional toolbar icons or open a **Favorites**, **History**, or **Feeds** pane by selecting one from the **Tools**, **Toolbars** sub-menu. This places a tick '√' character on the selected options. Selecting them again, will toggle the options off. The middle toolbar buttons only appear if you have Adobe and Norton installed.

Favorites

Using Favorites (their spelling, not ours) which are a kind of Bookmarks, is an easy way to access the Web pages that you need to visit on a regular basis. It is much easier

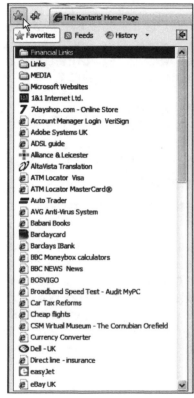

to select a page URL address from a sorted list, than to look it up and manually type it into the Address field. With **Internet Explorer**, a 'Favorite' is simply a Windows shortcut to a Web page.

When you first use **Internet Explorer** there may already be some **Favorites** available for you to use. Later, as your list of regular sites grows, your **Favorites** menu structure will grow too.

Fig. 10.9 The Favorites List.

With **Explorer 7** there are two ways of accessing your list of **Favorites**: From the **Favorites Center**, as shown above, by clicking the **Favorites** toolbar button shown here, or by using the **Tools**, **Toolbars** sub-menu and clicking the **Favorites** option. The latter method opens the **Favorites** list into a separate pane, on the left of the Explorer window, which remains open until you close it.

Adding a Favorite

There are several ways to add a 'Favorite' to the menu. When you are viewing a Web page that you want to visit again, the easiest method is to right-click on the page and select **Add to Favorites** from the displayed menu, as shown in Fig. 10.10 below.

Fig. 10.10 Using the Object Menu.

Another way is to use the **Add to Favorites** ⚜ toolbar button and select the **Add to Favorites** menu option as shown in Fig. 10.11.

Fig. 10.11 The Add to Favorites Menu.

Both methods start the same procedure by opening the Add a Favorite dialogue box shown in Fig. 10.12. In this dialogue box you can give the URL to the desired Web site a name of your choice, then click the **Add** button to complete the procedure.

Fig. 10.12 The Add Favorites Dialogue Box.

History Files

Internet Explorer stores all the Web pages and files you view on your hard disc, and places temporary pointers to them in a folder. To return to these in the future, click the **History** option from the **Favorites Center** sub-menu, shown here, which opens the **History** list shown in Fig. 10.13 below.

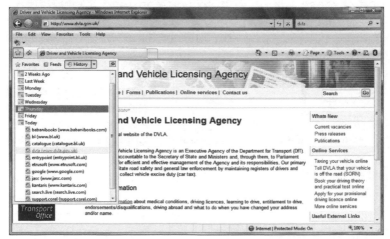

Fig. 10.13 Using the History Bar.

As with the **Favorites** list, the **History** list can also be opened in its own pane by using the **Tools**, **Toolbars** sub-menu and clicking the **History** option.

If you are not using a Broadband connection to the Internet, but pay for your Internet access by the minute, you can profit from browsing history files offline. To do so, first click the **Tools** toolbar icon and select the **Menu Bar** option from the drop-down menu. This adds a **Menu** bar to the Explorer Window, as shown here, from

which you can use the **File**, **Work Offline** menu command.

In this way, you can scroll offline through the sites you have recently visited, without having to read Web pages when they are live. Do make sure, however, that such pages have completely downloaded, so that you can work through them at your leisure.

Clicking on a site on the **History** list will open a sub-list of all the pages you accessed there, and selecting one of these will open it so you can read it whether on line or offline. You can do the same thing by right-clicking

on any list item which gives you the options to **Expand** or **Collapse** the list, or to **Delete** it, as shown here. This last option allows you to edit out any pages you don't want to keep in the list.

The length of time history items are kept on your hard disc can be controlled by clicking the **Tools** toolbar icon and selecting the **Internet Options** menu option which displays the tabbed dialogue box shown in Fig. 10.14.

Clicking the **Settings** button opens an additional

Fig. 10.14 The Internet Options.

dialogue box in which you can select the number of days that **History** files are kept. To delete all history items click the **Delete** button in the Internet Options dialogue box which will release the hard disc space used.

Web Feeds

Web feeds (feeds for short), also known as RSS (which stands for Really Simple Syndication, used to describe the technology used in creating feeds), contain frequently updated content published by a Web site. They are usually used for news and blogs (Web logs), but are also used for distributing other types of digital content, including pictures, audio or video.

You use feeds if you want to keep in touch with what interests you, but don't have the time to spend browsing through lots of Web sites to find out what is new. Web feeds allow you to take, for example, headlines from a lot of sites and collate them into Internet Explorer 7, or Microsoft Outlook 2007.

To gather information on a specific subject, all you have to do is visit the Web sites which contain it and check that the feed symbol in the toolbar of Internet Explorer is orange (if it is grey there is no feed option on that Web site).

To add a feed into Internet Explorer, click the feed symbol on the site section which interests you. To get content automatically, you will be expected to subscribe to a feed. When you click the orange feed symbol on a Web site, a separate window is displayed with all the feeds on the chosen Web site. This allows you to check you are subscribing to the right feed. Clicking **Subscribe to this feed**, adds your selection to the Explorer's **Favorites** list.

When you subscribe to a feed, it is added to the **Common Feed List**. Updated information from the feed is automatically downloaded to your computer and can be viewed in **Internet Explorer 7**, **Microsoft Outlook 2007**, or **Windows Media Center**. You can then filter the downloaded information by date, or subject matter.

The Cache

If you have used a previous version of **Internet Explorer**, you may have noticed that a Web page, especially one with lots of graphics, loads more quickly if you had already viewed it recently. This is because all the pages and files you view are stored either in the **History** folder or in a cache folder on your hard disc, called **Temporary Internet** files. The next time you access that page, depending on your settings, **Explorer** checks to see if the page has been updated before bringing it to the screen. If any change to the page has occurred, the new version is downloaded. If not, a cached copy is quickly retrieved.

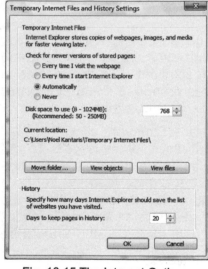

Internet **Explorer 7** assumes that you are using a Broadband connection, therefore its default setting for **Browsing history** is to reload every Web page you visit afresh. To alter this setting, click the **Settings** button on the **Browsing history** section of the General tabbed sheet shown in Fig. 10.14 to open the dialogue box shown in Fig. 10.15.

Fig. 10.15 The Internet Options.

As with the **History** files, you control the cache from the Internet Options dialogue box. The **Browsing history** section of the General settings tabbed sheet is shown in Fig. 10.14 on the previous page. Pressing the **Delete** button will clear the cache, which will very rapidly free up space on your hard disc.

Finally, in the **Home page** section of the **Internet Options** dialogue box of Fig. 10.14, you can choose which Web site is displayed when you first start **Internet Explorer**. To change it to one of your choice, type its URL in the text box, then click the **Apply** button. In this way, when you start **Internet Explorer** (or click the **Home** toolbar button, shown here, while connected to the Internet), the Web page of your choice will be displayed. You can also have a blank page loaded on starting the **Explorer**. The choice is yours!

Tabbed Browsing

Tabbed browsing is made possible for the first time with the introduction of **Internet Explorer 7**. This means that you can now open several Web sites in one Explorer window and switch between them by clicking on their tab. To create a new tab, click the **New Tab** icon, pointed to in Fig. 10.16, immediately to the right of an open Web page.

Fig. 10.16 The New Tab Icon.

What displays next is shown in Fig. 10.17 on the next page.

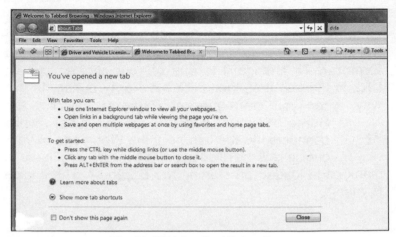

Fig. 10.17 Using the History Bar.

Note that the link '**about:Tabs**' is highlighted which means that you can simply type a new Web address, or you can click the **Favorites Center** icon and select a Web site from the **Favorites** list. Also note that whichever tab is active, an 'x' is displayed after its name, which can be clicked to close that tab.

Using Quick Tabs

To illustrate the use of **Quick Tabs** we use the **New Tab** icon to open several Web sites, all to do with banks as shown in Fig. 10.18, because we would like to compare their interest rates.

Fig. 10.18 The New Tab Icon.

Note that when more that one tab is used a new button appears between the first tab and the **Add to Favorites** button. This is the **Quick Tabs** button which when clicked displays all the tabbed Web sites, as shown in Fig. 10.19.

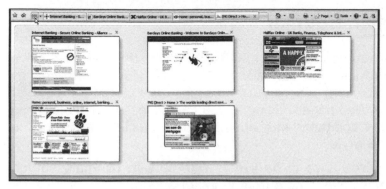

Fig. 10.19 The Quick Tabs Display.

Clicking the **Quick Tabs** button again, displays the contents of the last tab.

Saving and Opening a Group of Tabs

To save a group of tabs, click the **Add to Favorites** button, then select the **Add Tab Group to Favorites** from the displayed list and give the group a name, as shown in Fig. 10.20 and click the **Add** button.

Fig. 10.20 The Favorites Centre Dialogue Box.

To open a group of tabs, click the **Favorites Center** button, click the folder you want to open, and click the arrow to the right of the folder name to open all the tabbed sites in the group.

To close all tabs simultaneously, click the **Close** button on the **Internet Explorer** screen.

msn Hotmail

If you don't have a mail account with an Internet Service Provider you can always use **msn Hotmail** (owned by Microsoft), where your messages are stored on a server as Web pages. Using it, you can access your e-mail from any computer with an Internet connection, anywhere in the world.

You have to be live to sign up with **Hotmail**, so you may have to do it from work, or a friend's PC, or a Cyber Cafe. You can't do this any more from Windows Mail itself, so open the **Internet Explorer** and enter the following URL into the Address box:

www.hotmail.com

This opens the **Hotmail** home page shown in Fig. 10.21.

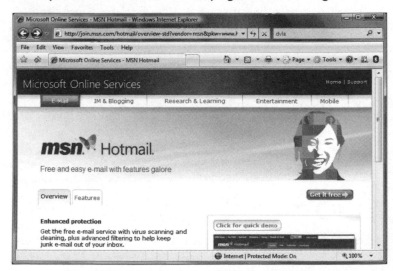

Fig. 10.21 The msn Hotmail Opening Web Page.

For a description of **Hotmail's** facilities you can use the **Click for quick demo** link near the bottom of the screen.

Next, click the **Get it free** link, which should open a registration options screen similar to the one in Fig 10.22.

Fig. 10.22 Activating your msn Hotmail Account.

Fill in this form carefully, including the text box asking you to type in the characters shown in the picture box (a security measure), without typing any spaces and click the **I Accept** button at the bottom of the form.

In our case and after only a few minutes we were registered and presented with the **Sign In** screen in Fig. 10.23 on the next page.

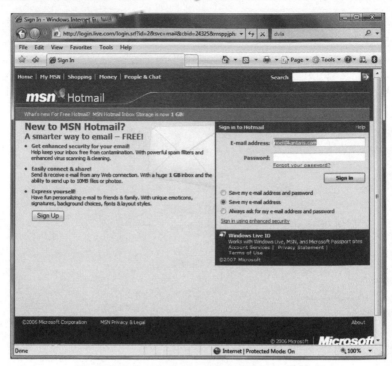

Fig. 10.23 Our Individual Hotmail Home Page.

That's as far as we will go with Hotmail. If you are interested, you can explore and learn more by using the e-mail features.

We suggest you set your **Hotmail** home page as one of your **Favorites**, or even your own home page. That way it will be very easy to access it in the future. You could also use it to carry on with your Web surfing when you have checked your messages. Good luck.

Explorer Help

Internet Explorer 7 has a built-in **Help** system which is

accessed by clicking the **Help** toolbar button shown here and selecting the **Contents and Index** option from the drop-down menu as shown in Fig. 10.24.

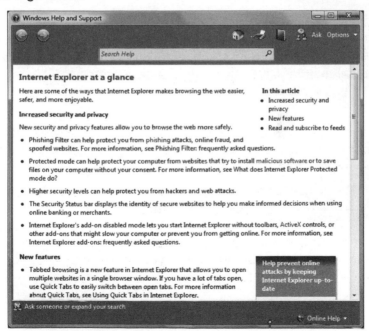

Fig. 10.24 The Help Menu Options.

This opens a Windows Help and Support window shown in Fig. 10.25.

Fig. 10.25 The Windows Help and Support Screen.

Another way of browsing the **Help** system is to use its **Search** facility to find specific topics. You can also access product support from Microsoft by clicking the **Help** toolbar button and selecting the **Online Support** option from the drop-down menu and following the available links.

We strongly recommend that you spend some time browsing through the **Help** topics listed above. You will learn a lot!

* * *

In the next chapter we discuss the Windows Media Player which can be used to play organise and play your digital media files, including music, videos, CDs, and DVDs.

* * *

11

Windows Media Player

You can use **Windows Media Player 11** to play and organise digital media files on your computer and from the Internet. In addition, you can use the Player to play, rip, and burn CDs; play DVDs and VCDs; and synchronise your music, videos, and your favourite recorded TV shows to portable devices, such as portable digital audio players, Pocket PCs, and Portable Media Centres.

Whether all the features described in this chapter work on your PC will depend on your system. Most of them require at least a CD-ROM player and a sound card and speakers to be fitted and correctly set up.

Starting the Media Player

The **Windows Media Player** can be opened by selecting ▶ Windows Media Player   its entry, shown here, on the **Start**, **All Programs** menu list which opens the Player. In our case, the first thing that happened was that the Player connected automatically to the Internet (we have a Broadband connection), and displayed the screen shown in Fig. 11.1 on the next page.

You can spend a lot of time watching film trailers or whole videos, some good, some definitely bad! Just point to a picture and when the mouse pointer changes to a hand, click the left mouse button to start playing. You get better visual definition if the Player's window is not too large.

Fig. 11.1 The Windows Media Player Screen after Connecting to the Internet.

Fig. 11.1 above, displays the Player in **Full Mode** in its own window (more about this shortly).

Playing Audio CDs

To start our introduction to the **Windows Media Player**, select one of your audio CDs and insert it in the CD-ROM drive of your PC. Windows Vista detects the CD and, if this is the first time you have inserted an audio CD in the PC's CD-ROM drive, it will display a dialogue box with a list of options, amongst which is to play this CD using **Windows Media Player**.

If the audio CD does not start in **Windows Media Player**, then use the **Start**, **Control Panel** menu command and, in **Classic View**, double-click the **AutoPlay** icon pointed to in Fig. 11.2 overleaf, to open the dialogue box shown in Fig. 11.3 where you can select the **Windows Media Player** as your preferred Player.

Fig. 11.2 The Control Panel in Classic View.

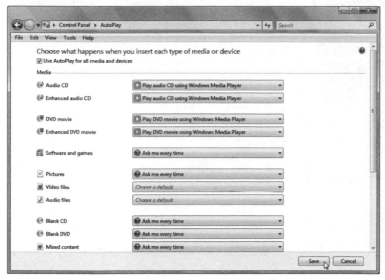

Fig. 11.3 The AutoPlay Dialogue Box.

Once the choice to use **Windows Media Player** has been made, all subsequent attempts to play an audio CD immediately start playing in **Windows Media Player**, as shown in Fig. 11.4 on the next page.

When the Player starts, it displays the **Now Playing** feature and scans the CD for unique identifying information, and if you are connected to the Internet it searches the Internet where music lists are stored for the majority of CDs published in the world. The retrieved data is then stored on your PC so you don't have to enter the track or artist information. Some CDs will download disc art such as the CD cover picture and display it as the CD plays. All of these features are shown in Fig. 11.4.

Fig. 11.4 Windows Media Player Screen Layout.

At any time if you double-click another track in the **Play List** it starts that track on the CD playing.

Apart from the online database, the Player acts just like an ordinary CD player that you control by clicking buttons, as shown in **Compact Mode** in Fig. 11.5 on the next page.

Clicking the **Switch to Compact Mode** button (see Fig. 11.4 on the previous page) displays the screen in Fig. 11.5 below.

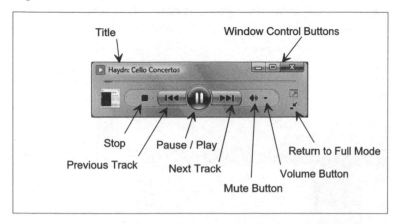

Fig. 11.5 The Player in Compact Mode Showing Button Controls.

The **Compact Mode** view does not show a screen at all, just the playing, mode change, and window control buttons, but it takes up much less room on your screen.

The Player has **Play**, **Pause**, **Stop**, **Previous Track**, and **Next Track** buttons, plus **Volume** and **Mute** controls. Moving the pointer over a button opens a pop-up Help box that describes what the button does.

In **Full Mode** you can adjust the sound volume with the **Volume Slider** to the right of the **Play** controls, while in the **Compact Mode** you'll have to click the **Volume** button to reveal the **Volume Slider** first before you can control the volume.

When you are finished you can select the **Play**, **Eject** menu command to stop playing and eject the CD from your drive, or more simply, just close the Player by clicking its **Close** ▬ button, but then you will have to eject the CD manually.

Notice there is no **Menu bar** shown in Fig. 11.4. It is available whenever you need it, by clicking the **Alt** key on the keyboard or right-clicking the **Features bar**. In Fig. 11.6 we show the shortcut **Menu bar** displaying with the **View** sub-menu open.

Fig. 11.6 The Player's Menu Bar.

If you want **Media Player** to show its **Menu bar** all the time, just select the **Classic Menus** option of the **View** menu command or use the **Ctrl+M** keyboard shortcut.

The **Tools**, **Options** command displays a multi-tab dialogue box in which, amongst other capabilities, you can customise your updates and the player settings. It is worthwhile having a look.

Fig. 11.6 above, shows some of the Player's features when in **Full Mode**. These change depending on the mode you are in and what the Player is actually doing at the time, but we have to start somewhere!

Skin Mode

We will now investigate the various 'skins' available in **Windows Media Player**, but before doing so, it might be worthwhile fixing the display of the **Menu bar** on the Player. Next, use the **View**, **Skin Mode** menu command, or **Ctrl+2**, to display the Player in **Skin Mode** as shown in Fig. 11.7 below.

Fig. 11.7 Mini Player Mode Controls.

Skin mode is an alternate and usually smaller view of the Player. It has fewer controls than Full Mode and does not openly display as much information while playing. The screen part of the window, as shown above, displays 'visualisations' that move in time to the music being played. These can be changed when in **Full Mode** by clicking the **Now Playing** button (see Fig. 11.4 on page 214), selecting **Visualisation** from the drop-down menu, then selecting, say, **Bars and Waves**, and finally choosing one of the available options, as shown in Fig. 11.8 on the next page.

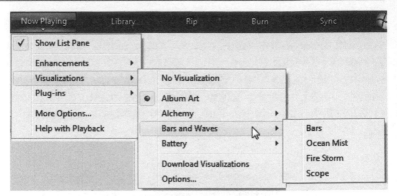

Fig. 11.8 The Visualizations Sub-menus.

You can return to **Full Mode** by clicking the **Switch to full mode** 🖫 button pointed to in Fig. 11.7 on the previous page, or using the **Ctrl+1** keyboard shortcut.

Choosing Skins

With **Windows Media Player** you can use the **View**, **Skin Chooser** menu command to display a list of available skins. The default skin is the **Corporate**, but you can select any one on the list and click the **Apply skin** ⟨Apply Skin⟩ button to make the selected skin active.

You can even get additional skins from the Internet by clicking the **More Skins** ⟨More Skins⟩ button. You will be amazed at the number of available skins. There are so

many that an A to Z grouping, as shown here, is included on the Internet Explorer's screen!

In Fig. 11.9 on the next page, we show a composite screen dump displaying all six skins on the same screen so you can see at a glance what is being offered. You, of course, will only see one skin at a time. When you find the one you like, don't forget to click the **Apply skin** ⟨Apply Skin⟩ button.

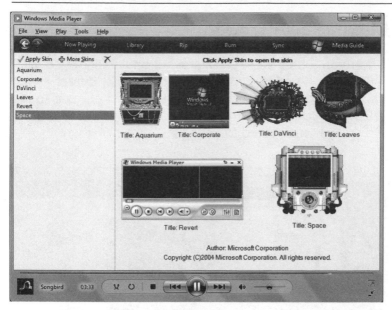

Fig. 11.9 Playing a Video File with Video Settings Open.

The Revert Skin

The skin we use most often when playing CDs or the Radio is the Revert skin. The Player can be minimised onto the Task bar in the usual way, but when maximised its window appears faded on the screen. When the mouse pointer is placed on the faded window, it lights up and displays as shown in Fig. 11.10. All the Player controls shown can be used to find and play your music.

Fig. 11.10 The Player in Revert Skin.

Most of the play control buttons are the same as those shown in Fig. 11.5 on page 215, so are not identified again here. We suggest you hover the mouse pointer over the new buttons to see their function. For example there is a **Quick Access Panel** button, a **Shuffle** and **Repeat** button, and **Graphic Equalizer** and **Playlist** buttons.

Playing a DVD or Video

When you insert a DVD (Digital Versatile Disc) into your DVD drive, Windows Media Player should detect it and start playing the introductory tracks (if not, see page 212). You control the movie just as you would a regular DVD player connected to your TV.

Fig. 11.11 Playing a DVD.

In our example above, we are about to start playing a film on DVD. On the right pane the disc's **Chapters** that you can jump to straight away are displayed. This was achieved by selecting **Show List Pane** from the **Now Playing** list. To start the film click the **Play** button.

Apart from pre-recorded films, you can use **Windows Media Player** to play and manipulate your own videos.

Playing a Media File

At any time you can select a new or different file to play using the **File** menu command. Use the **Open** option from the displayed sub-menu for a file stored on your computer, navigate to the appropriate location, click the file, and then click **Open**. Use the **File, Open URL** menu command for an Internet file, type the URL to the file, and then click **OK**, or browse your network for an audio or video file which can then be added to your library. To play a streaming media file on a Web page just click the link on the Web page.

The video shown in Fig. 11.12 is playing in the **Enhancements** mode selected from the **Now Playing** list, and displays the **Graphic Equalizer**.

Fig. 11.12 Playing a Video File – Crossing the Corinth Canal.

The various 'presets' can be used to fine tune your video recordings. For example, you can change the colour, brightness, contrast and zoom settings of your video image. You can cycle through several other settings panes with the ◀ and ▶ buttons. These give you controls to adjust such things as graphic-equaliser levels, audio effects, play speed, and the colour of your **Media Player**. When you are happy with your settings click the ✖ button to close the pane.

When the Player opens with a video or DVD, it automatically adjusts its size to give optimum resolution and picture quality. You can, though, set it to any size you want. One way is to drag the bottom-right corner of the Player window. As the window size changes, so does the playing image area inside it.

The Features Bar

The streamlined buttons displayed on the top of the **Media Player** when in **Full Mode** (see Fig. 11.12) make up the **Features bar**. The functions of these buttons are:

 Shows information about the content that is playing, or displays a visualisation, video or DVD.

 Lets you organise and access the digital media files on your computer and links to content on the Internet, or creates playlists.

 Rips, or copies, selected tracks from a CD and saves them to the library on your computer.

 Lets you make up your own CDs from tracks you have stored on your PC.

Synchronises music, videos, and recorded TV shows to portable devices, such as portable digital audio players, Pocket PCs, and Portable Media Centres.

Accesses the online Radio and other digital media on the Internet.

Ripping a CD

Ripping from a CD is not as destructive as it sounds. It simply means copying tracks from the CD to the library on your computer hard disc, so that you can listen to them whenever you are working. To rip tracks from an audio CD, put the CD into the drive which will display a screen similar to the one in Fig. 11.13 below.

Fig. 11.13 Playing an Audio CD and Displaying Album Information.

Clicking the **Rip** button on the **Features bar** displays the screen in Fig. 11.14.

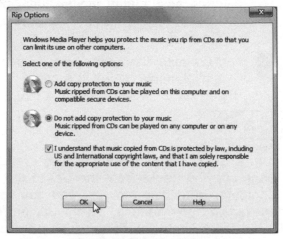

Fig. 11.14 The Rip Options.

Once you've chosen from the options and clicked the **OK** button, the Rip page with all the album tracks named and selected is displayed as shown in Fig. 11.15.

Fig. 11.15 Preparing for the Rip Procedure.

If there are any tracks that you do not want to rip, clear the check box next to them. When you are ready, click the **Start Rip** 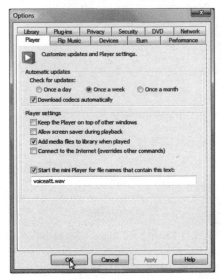 button to start the process.

By default the selected tracks are copied to the **Music** folder on your PC and can then be displayed in the **Library** feature. Sub-folders will be added and labelled with the name of the artist or group. Further, you can change the folder where your music files are stored in the Rip Music tabbed sheet of the Options dialogue box, shown in Fig. 11.16 below. This is opened with the **Tools**, **Options** command.

Fig. 11.16 Controlling Rip Music Settings in the Options Box.

While the ripping operation is in progress you can see exactly what is going on by looking at the Rip Status column, shown empty in Fig. 11.15. You can listen to the CD while you are ripping it, so you needn't get too bored. To cancel the operation at any time just click the **Stop Rip** button.

The Library

The first time you use this option by clicking the **Library** button on the **Features bar**, the **Media Player** searches your system for audio and video files and then displays a screen similar to that in Fig. 11.17 below. At any time you can force a similar search with the **File**, **Add to Library** command.

Fig. 11.17 Finding our Ripped CD in the Library.

As you can see from the **Library** drop-down sub-menu, the Player searches and categorises **Music**, **Pictures**, and **Video** files separately. Selecting one of these sub-menu lists displays more information on its contents. In our example above, you can see where the album added in the last section was placed. Double-clicking on a track title starts playing that track.

Creating a New Playlist

If you click the **Library** button, and select **Create Play List** from the opened menu, you can create a new playlist which opens in a pane on the right side of the Player, shown below. A Playlist is a list of tracks from one or more albums in your music library. You may want to create a playlist of your party favourites to save to a CD or other portable device. Playlists can contain tracks from any album on your hard disc.

Fig. 11.18 Dragging Album Tracks onto a New Playlist.

Above, we show a music track being dragged into the List pane to add it to the new playlist. When you have selected what you want to make up your playlist, click the **Save Playlist** button, and type a name to replace the

default highlighted **Untitled Playlist** (in our example we named it **ABBA Selection**). The new playlist is added to the Playlists and can be manipulated as shown here in the drop-down menu.

Burning Files to a CD

You use the **Burn** function to transfer media files from your PC to a CD. In this way you can customise a CD for say, using in your car CD player on your next long trip. To do this you will obviously need a CD drive that is capable of burning CDs. To start the process, first click the **Burn** button on the **Feature bar** to open a Player display similar to the one below.

Fig. 11.19 Selecting Files to Burn to a CD.

Put a blank CD in your CD recorder, and click the **Burn** button and select **'Now Playing' List to Drive E:** option from the sub-menu pointed to in Fig. 11.19 above. Your drive letter could be different.

Note the option to burn to an **Audio CD** is preselected. You also have the option to burn to a **Data CD or DVD**. Selecting these options is dependent on your drive and the type of CD you put in it, as follows:

Audio CD   Creates music CDs similar to the ones you buy. The Player converts tracks from the music playlists in your library into **.cda** files, and then burns them to the compact disc. They can be played in most computers, and CD players.

Data CD   Creates CDs to back up the digital media files and playlists in your library. Only certain CD players and computers can play them.

Click the **Start Burn** button to convert the files and create your new CD. You can copy tracks either to a recordable CD (CD-R) or a rewritable CD (CD-RW). With CD-Rs, you can copy tracks only once. With CD-RWs, you can copy tracks many times, but you must erase the disc before you can use the Player to copy new tracks.

The Sync Option

You use the **Sync** option to transfer media from your PC to portable devices, such as palm-size PCs, mobile phones, or other portable music devices.

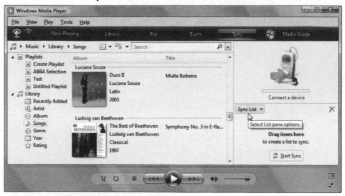

Fig. 11.20 The Sync Option on the Features Bar.

This procedure (see Fig. 11.20 on the previous page) is very similar to the **Burn** function, just covered, except that you have to create a 'partnership' between the Media Player and your device. It is worth looking at the **Help with Sync** sub-menu option which displays when the down-arrow of the **Sync** button is clicked.

If you need to, we suggest you explore this topic on your own.

* * *

In Chapter 12 we discuss how to work with images and show you how to organise your photos using the Windows Photo Gallery. We also introduce the Windows Movie Maker which you can use to edit and rearrange your home-made video cam movies.

* * *

12

Working with Images

Using a Camera or Scanner

If your digital camera or scanner are Plug-and-Play,

Fig. 12.1 The AutoPlay Screen.

Windows Vista will detect them (if connected to your PC) and will display the AutoPlay screen shown in Fig. 12.1. To start the procedure, click the **Import pictures** option.

If your camera or scanner is not Plug-and-Play, use the **Start**, **Control Panel** menu option and double-click the **Scanners and Cameras** icon shown here in **Classic View**.

The **Scanners and Cameras** Wizard will guide you through the process. You might be asked for the disc that came with the device so that its driver can be installed. It is possible, however, that you might need to get the latest driver that is compatible with Windows Vista, by looking at your hardware manufacturer's Web site. In our case, for example, the manufacturers of our scanner are not planning to issue a new driver for it – too old they say!

Selecting the **Import pictures** option on the AutoPlay screen, displays the Importing Pictures and Videos dialogue box in Fig. 12.2, in which you can type a tag for the folder in which the pictures will be placed. By default, the folder will be created in the **Pictures** folder with the current date (and tag) as its name.

Fig. 12.2 The Importing Pictures and Videos Screen.

Clicking the **Import** button, starts the process, as shown in Fig. 12.3 below, which is very fast indeed – a few seconds from starting the job is done.

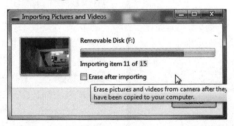

Fig. 12.3 The Importing Pictures and Videos Process.

As you can see in Fig. 12.3, you even have the option to delete the pictures from the camera after they have been copied to your computer. On completion of the import procedure, the pictures are opened in **Windows Photo Gallery**, as shown in Fig. 12.4 on the next page.

Note that some pictures were taken by turning the camera to an upright position, but can be turned back by 90° to view them the right way up, by using the rotating buttons provided at the bottom of the Windows Photo Gallery window.

Fig. 12.4 The Windows Photo Gallery.

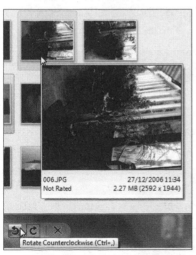

Fig. 12.5 Rotating a Picture.

The first thing to be done here is to rotate the pictures which lie on their side to an upright position. To do this, hover with the mouse pointer over each such picture, which enlarges it, as shown in Fig. 12.5, then left-click it to select it (you will see small dots surrounding the selected picture), and click the **Anticlockwise** button to rotate it the right way up.

If you find that you don't like some pictures, deleting them is easy; just select them, then click the **Delete** ✕ button.

The Windows Photo Gallery

The **Windows Photo Gallery** can also be opened from the **Start**, **All Programs** menu. The program makes it easy to view, organise, edit, e-mail, burn to CD, and print digital pictures, whether these have come from a camera or a scanner.

By default, **Windows Photo Gallery** shows all the pictures and videos that are located in the **Pictures**

folder, as shown here, with a choice to see the Pictures or the Videos separately. You can also add other folders to this scheme which is useful as you might have photos and videos in folders other than the **Pictures** folder.

Pictures and videos are categorised under the dates taken, as shown in Fig. 12.6, and can also be found with the search facility by typing appropriate criteria, such as filename, tag, and date taken, in the Search box.

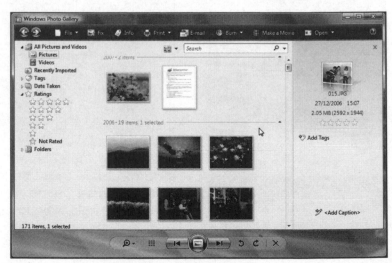

Fig. 12.6 Pictures Categorised by Date Taken.

Previewing an Image

If you double-click an image or select **Preview Picture** from its right-click menu, then that image is displayed enlarged in the **Windows Photo Gallery**, as shown in Fig. 12.7 below.

Fig. 12.7 The Windows Photo Gallery Preview.

Note the buttons at the bottom of the screen. You can use these to navigate through your pictures folder, select the viewing size, view the pictures in your folder as a slide show, zoom in or out, rotate the image, and generally carry out certain housekeeping functions. You can, for example, use the toolbar icons to **Fix**, **Print**, **E-mail**, **Burn** to CD/DVD, or **Make a Movie** which opens the **Microsoft Movie Maker**.

The **Windows Photo Gallery** can of course be used with other image documents including Fax documents or scanned pictures, as indicated in the information given on the above picture – it is the Welcome Scan picture provided by Microsoft and comes with Vista.

The Slide Show View

To see your photos in another interesting display, click

the centre button of the navigation bar at the bottom of the **Photo Gallery** screen shown here.

You can use the **Slide Show** facility with any folder that contains pictures. Just double-click on one of the pictures in the folder, then click the **Slide Show** button on the displayed **Photo Gallery** – it will just go on showing the pictures within the selected folder in full screen, as shown in Fig. 12.8 below.

Fig. 12.8 Photos Displayed in Slide Show View.

When you have enough, you can switch off the **Slide Show** by pressing the **Esc** key on the keyboard.

If you move the mouse pointer onto the area of a slide show, the **Slide Show Controls** are displayed, as shown in Fig. 12.9 on the next page.

These **Slide Show Controls** have the indicated functions.

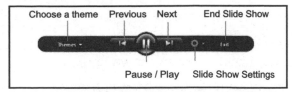

Fig. 12.9 The Slide Show Controls.

The Windows Movie Maker

With **Windows Movie Maker** you can edit and rearrange your home-made video cam movies, make a shorter version of them, add a still picture and voice over, and either post them to your Web site for all to see, or send them as an attachment to an e-mail to your friends.

The **Movie Maker** can be found in the **All Programs** listing. Clicking its icon, starts the program and displays a screen similar to Fig. 12.10.

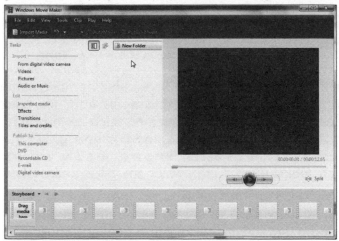

Fig. 12.10 The Windows Movie Maker Screen.

The displayed screen is divided into four panes, with the left pane showing the available **Tasks**. To the right of this pane, the folder holding your video collection will be displayed when you select it from the **Videos** folder. Windows automatically created this folder during installation, named it **Videos**, and placed within it any video films that it found on your PC, as shown below.

Fig. 12.11 The Windows Movie Maker Video Folder.

The three video clips shown here came as video samples with Windows Vista. Note that apart from the **Videos** folder, you also have other folders, such as the **Pictures** and **Audio or Music** folders, the contents of which can be used for perhaps assembling a slide show with added music, fading effects, etc., which we will examine shortly.

We will start, however, with the rather short **Bear** video which we will break up into frames, and edit it by removing unwanted parts of it that might be spoiling it.

To start, select the **Bear** clip in Fig. 12.11 and click the **Import** button to insert it in the **Movie Maker** screen, as shown in Fig. 12.12 below.

At the top of the Movie Maker screen there is the usual selection of menu options and toolbar icons, while at the bottom of the screen is the **Workspace** area. It is here that you assemble your movie, which can be viewed either as a 'timeline' (focuses on timing) or 'storyboard' (focuses on sequencing) view.

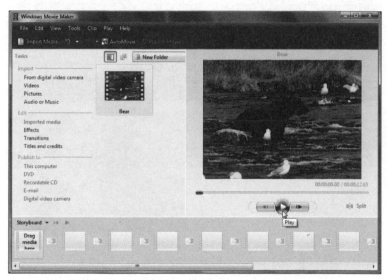

Fig. 12.12 The Windows Movie Maker Screen.

In the timeline view, you can synchronise video clips with audio clips or create fading transitions between clips with the help of a number of tools that appear at the far left of the **Workspace** area.

Start this video by clicking the **Play** button below the **Preview** pane. If you continue watching it you will come across several frames in which an alarmed seagull takes off and its wing obscures the face of the bear.

We are only using this as an example of how to remove such offending frames from a video. After all, it could be a waving hand that momentarily obscured a bride's face in a wedding video and spoiled the whole precious moment!

In Fig. 12.13, we first switched to the **Timeline** view, then dragged the imported video onto it. Next, we played the video, but stopped it at the first offending place. We then used the **Previous Frame** and **Next Frame** controls under the **Preview** pane to move the video a fraction of a second before the offending instance, then clicked the **Split** button.

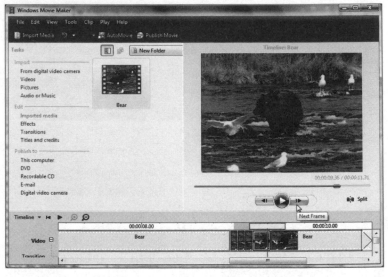

Fig. 12.13 Stopping a Video on an Unwanted Frame.

We continued in this way from frame to frame splitting the video just before and just after the seagull's left wing obscured the face of the bear. Finally, we removed all the offending frames by right-clicking them and selecting **Remove** from the drop-down menu.

To combine clips, on the timeline select the remaining ones, and use the **Clip**, **Combine** menu option.

To save your creation, use the **File**, **Save Project As** menu command and give the project a name. We called it **Bear2**.

Fig. 12.14 Saving a Video Project.

Creating a Slide Show

You can use **Movie Maker** to create a slide show. As an example we will use some of the pictures in the **Sample Pictures** folder that came with Windows Vista. In Fig. 12.15, shown on the next page, we have selected five pictures with a common theme – water.

To rearrange the sequence of your creation, drag the pictures in the sequence you want them to appear in your slide show onto the **Workspace** area.

You can import an audio file that plays while the slide show is actually displaying, and also include 'transitions' between pictures so that you do not have abrupt changes from one picture to the other. To do this, switch to **Timeline** view and use the various **Edit** options in the **Tasks** pane by dragging them on the area between the pictures. Also try using the **3D Ripple** effect – it would simulate a swimming turtle! We leave it to you to experiment – you will enjoy the result!

Fig. 12.15 Producing a Slide Show with Movie Maker.

Sending a Movie as an E-mail Attachment

Some digital cameras have the facility of recording short video clips of 15-30 seconds duration in audio video interleaved (**.avi**) format – it interleaves waveform audio and digital video. These are fun to watch on your computer, but rather large (2.5-4.5 MB) in size to send as an attachment to friends or relatives. Such files cannot be shrunk in the way scanned or digital camera pictures can, but there is a way of dealing with the problem.

To shrink such an audio video file, start **Windows Movie Maker** and import the **Bear** video. The program is loaded and displays on your screen. Next, drag it to the **Workspace** area, as shown in Fig. 12.16 on the next page.

Fig. 12.16 The Movie Maker Screen.

To see the size of the imported video (it is 3.86 MB) right-click its entry in the **Contents** pane to display Fig. 12.17 shown on the next page.

Finally, use the **File**, **Save Project As** menu command to display the Save Project As dialogue box and give your creation a name – we called it **Bear Movie**.

Fig. 12.17 The Properties Screen of the Import Video.

Next, navigate to where you saved your project (in our case this was in the **Videos** folder), and place the mouse pointer on the file to see its size on the displayed pop-up, as shown in Fig. 12.18 on the next page.

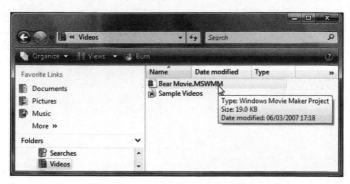

Fig. 12.18 The Smaller Size Bear Movie.

Note the difference in size; the original was 3.86 MB, while this one is only 19 KB! You can now send this file as a normal attachment to an e-mail, without making enemies of your friends! It is important that you save this file as we have indicated on the previous page, and not publishing it by using **Movie Maker's** other menu commands, as these will use the original file size and unless your friend is on Broadband you'll get into trouble!

* * *

In the next chapter we discuss the following topics: Accessibility, which helps users with visual or hearing difficulties; Mobility, which helps users with notebooks to manage power plans; Compatibility which helps users run programs which might be unstable in Windows Vista, but were running perfectly well under a previous version of Windows.

* * *

13

Accessibility, Mobility and Program Compatibility

In this chapter we will examine how you can adjust your PC's settings for vision, hearing, mobility, and program compatibility. We begin by using the **Start**, **Control Panel** menu command which displays the screen shown in Fig. 13.1 (in **Classic View**).

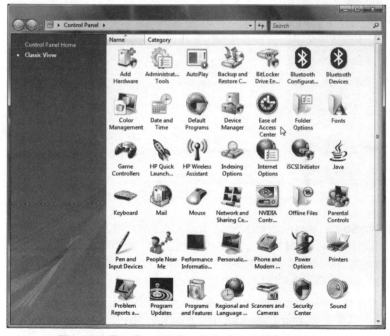

Fig. 13.1 The Control Panel Screen in Classic View.

If **Control Panel** displays in **Category View**, click the **Classic View** link.

In either **Control Panel** view, to start the **Easy Access Center**, click the icon shown here. In **Classic View**, this displays the screen below.

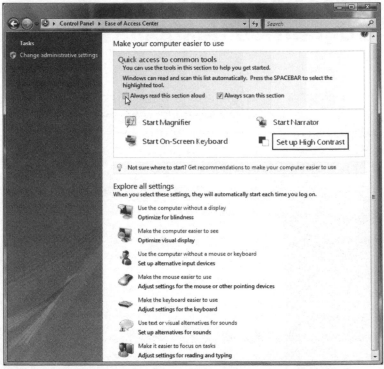

Fig. 13.2 The Easy Access Center Options Screen.

Windows Vista gives you the opportunity to make your PC more accessible to individuals who have difficulty typing or using a mouse, have slightly impaired vision, or are hard of hearing.

If the Narrator annoys you, click the box pointed to in Fig. 13.2 to remove the tick mark from it. While you are doing this, you might as well remove the tick mark from the adjacent box, 'Always scan this section', to stop the mouse focus from rotating between the four Start entries.

The Microsoft Magnifier

To start the Microsoft Magnifier, click the **Start Magnifier** words (not its icon) situated near the middle part of the screen, shown in Fig. 13.2.

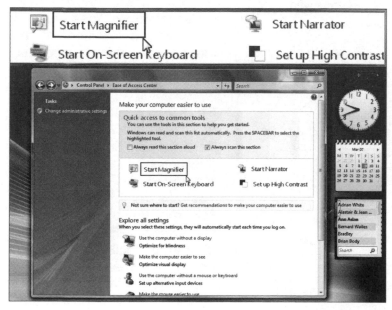

Fig. 13.3 The Magnifier Screen.

The displayed Magnifier screen is shown in Fig. 13.3 above. Note that wherever we place the mouse pointer on the actual (lower) screen, that part of the screen is magnified in a window at the top of the screen. The magnifying window can be made bigger by clicking on it, then moving the pointer to the lower edge of the window until the mouse pointer changes to a double-headed arrow and drag the edge down to make the window bigger. In some computers the shape of this arrow might be different – in ours it displays as a four-headed arrow!

Clicking the **Magnifier** icon on the **Taskbar**, shown here, opens the Magnifier dialogue box shown in Fig. 13.4.

From here you can set the **Scale factor** from 1 (low)

to 16 (high), select other **Presentation** options, such as the docking position of the Magnifier window, and set **Tracking** options.

Selecting **Minimize on Startup** under **Option**, minimises the **Magnifier** on the **Taskbar** next time you start the application. To now exit **Magnifier**, click its entry on the **Taskbar**, remove the minimise tick from the option, and click the **Close** ![X] button. The **Magnifier** facility is removed from your screen.

Fig. 13.4 The Magnifier Dialogue Box.

The On-Screen Keyboard

To activate the **On-Screen Keyboard**, click the **Start On-Screen Keyboard** words (not its icon) situated just below the **Start Magnifier** entry near the middle part of the screen shown in Fig. 13.2.

This displays the screen shown in Fig. 13.5 on the next page. The virtual keyboard allows users with mobility impairments to type data using a pointing device or joystick. The result is exactly as if you were using the actual keyboard.

Fig. 13.5 The On-Screen Virtual Keyboard.

The **On-Screen Keyboard** has three typing modes you can use to type data. These are:

- Clicking mode – you click the on-screen keys to type text.

- Hovering mode – you use a mouse or joystick to point to a key for a predefined period of time, and the selected character is typed automatically.

- Scanning mode – the **On-Screen Keyboard** continually scans the keyboard and highlights areas where you can type keyboard characters by pressing a hot key or using a switch-input device.

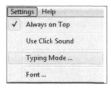

Fig. 13.6 The On-Screen Keyboard Settings Menu.

The three typing modes are selected by choosing the **Settings Typing Mode** menu command, as shown in Fig. 13.6. This opens the Typing Mode dialogue box shown in Fig. 13.7 in which you click the option you prefer and, if appropriate, the time interval before the command is actioned.

Fig. 13.7 The Typing Mode of the On-Screen Keyboard.

Also, note that you can select from the **Settings** menu to have the virtual keyboard appear **Always on Top** of all other windows displayed on your screen, and also select to **Use Click Sound** which is particularly useful if you are using the **Hover to select** option of **Typing Mode**.

There are several types of **On-Screen Keyboards** which are chosen from the **Keyboard** menu (Fig. 13.8). These are:

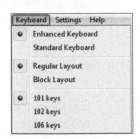

- The **Enhanced Keyboard** that includes the numeric keypad.

- The **Standard Keyboard** that does not include the numeric keypad.

Fig. 13.8 The Keyboard Menu of the On-Screen Keyboard.

You can also display the keyboard with the keys in the **Regular Layout**, or in a **Block Layout** (arranged in rectangular blocks). **Block Layout** is especially useful in scanning mode. Finally, you can select to display the US standard keyboard (**101 keys**), the universal keyboard (**102 keys**), or a keyboard with additional Japanese language characters (**106 keys**).

The Keyboard Options

Clicking the **Make the keyboard easier to use** link in Fig. 13.2, displays the screen shown in Fig. 13.9 on the next page. From here you can tick the **Turn on Sticky Keys** option, then click the **Set Up Sticky Keys** link to display an additional dialogue box (Fig. 13.10) which allows the user to press a modifier key, such as the **Shift** key 5 times, to activate the **Sticky Keys** option. This allows a user to press the keys **Ctrl**, **Alt**, and **Shift**, one at a time. This is useful to people who have difficulty pressing two or more keys at a time.

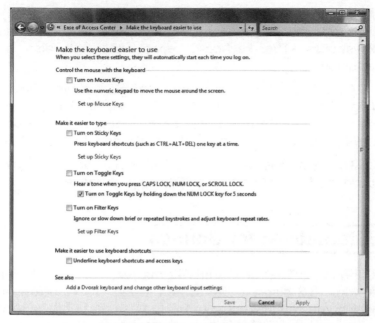

Fig. 13.9 Turning on Sticky Keys.

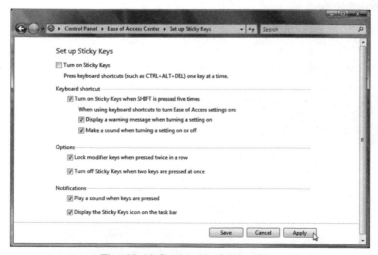

Fig. 13.10 Setting Up Sticky Keys.

Activating the **Turn on Filter Keys** option (Fig. 13.9), instructs the keyboard to ignore brief or repeated keystrokes. The keyboard repeat rate can also be adjusted.

Activating the **Turn on Toggle Keys** option (Fig. 13.9), instructs your PC to play a high-pitched sound when the **Caps Lock**, **Scroll Lock**, or **Num Lock** keys are on and a low-pitched sound when they are off.

The **Settings** buttons against each of the above options allow for fine tuning of these preferences.

Alternatives for Sounds

Clicking the **Text or Visual Alternatives for Sounds** link in Fig. 13.2 displays the screen in Fig. 13.11 below, in which you can instruct your PC to flash part of its screen every time the system's built-in speaker plays a sound. In addition, you can choose which part of the screen you want to flash.

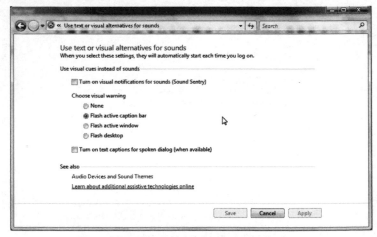

Fig. 13.11 Alternatives for Sounds Screen.

The Display Options

Activating the **Set up High Contrast** option, see Fig. 13.2, displays the screen shown in Fig. 13.12 below. On this screen you can instruct programs to change their colour-specific schemes to a **High Contrast** scheme specified by you. Fonts are also changed whenever possible to improve legibility.

You can also change the rate at which the insertion point blinks and its width by dragging the two sliders appropriately.

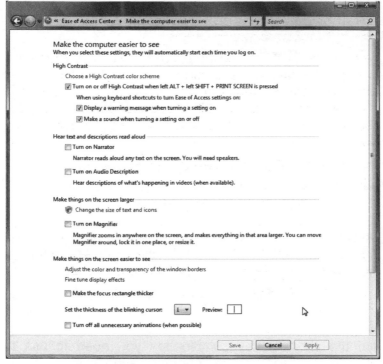

Fig. 13.12 The Display Options Screen.

The Mouse Options

Activating the **Make the mouse easier to use** link in Fig. 13.2, displays the screen in Fig. 13.13 below.

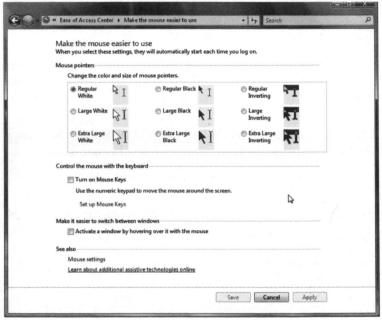

Fig. 13.13 The Mouse Options Screen.

On this screen you can change the colour and size of the mouse pointer, and control the mouse pointer's movements with the keys on the numeric keypad.

Clicking the **Set up Mouse Keys** link, displays an additional screen in which you can control, amongst other things, the speed at which the mouse pointer is moving, and the shortcut key combination you need to use to activate and deactivate the numeric keypad.

Power Plans and Mobility

The Windows **Power Plans** cater for three main power designs that can help you save energy, maximise system performance, or achieve a balance between the two. Not only can you change the default power plans supplied with Vista, but you can also build your own to suit your specific needs.

The default power plans should meet most user's needs, but if you need to build your own, then you can use one of the default power plans as a starting point.

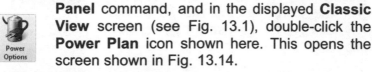

To see the default power plans, use the **Start**, **Control Panel** command, and in the displayed **Classic View** screen (see Fig. 13.1), double-click the **Power Plan** icon shown here. This opens the screen shown in Fig. 13.14.

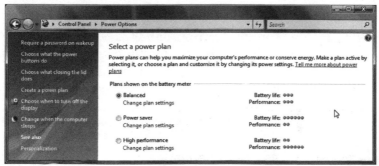

Fig. 13.14 The Power Options Screen.

The three default **Power Plans** provided by Windows are as follows:

Balanced: Giving good performance when it is needed, but saving power during periods of inactivity.

Power saver: Giving reduced performance, but decreasing dramatically power consumption. This plan is helpful to mobile users.

High performance: Giving maximum performance, but using far more power, making it rather unhelpful to mobile users.

All of these plans can be adapted by clicking on the appropriate **Change plan settings** link.

You can also change between the default plans because there is easy access to them directly from the Vista **System tray**, as shown here. You will have to click the **System tray** icon, pointed to on the screen of Fig. 13.15, to see what is displayed here. Hovering over the icon with the mouse pointer only tells you of the current power plan selection.

Fig. 13.15 The Power Plan Screen.

The Mobility Center

To display the **Mobility Center**, either click the last link in Fig. 13.15 above, or double-click the **Control Panel** icon shown here. Either of these actions displays a screen similar to the one shown in Fig. 13.16 below.

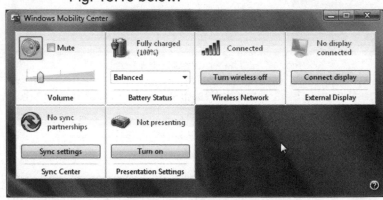

Fig. 13.16 The Mobility Center Screen of our Notebook.

The **Mobility Center** is a new application designed entirely for mobile PC users. It gives you instant access to all the **Wireless**, **Power**, **Synchronisation** and **Volume** settings, allowing you to change these at will and on the fly.

What you might notice in Fig. 13.16, is that two tiles (application elements) are missing from the **Mobility Center**. One is the **Display Brightness**, the other the **Screen Orientation**.

The **Screen Orientation** is relevant to Tablet PC users only, while the **Display Brightness** can be of relevance to Notebook users operating under certain conditions. For example, they might like to decrease display brightness so as to increase battery power.

If any of the tiles are missing from your **Mobility Center**, Microsoft suggests that it might be because of missing hardware or their drivers and suggest to contact the manufacturer of your mobile PC. This might be easier said than done. From our experience, all we can say regarding the availability of Windows Vista compatible hardware drivers is, 'be patient'. It might happen one day!

Program Compatibility

Program compatibility is a mode in Windows that lets you run programs written for earlier versions of Windows. Most programs written for Windows XP also work in Windows Vista, but some older programs might run poorly or not run at all. To correct this, use the **Program Compatibility Wizard** to simulate earlier versions of Windows.

Note: Do not use the **Program Compatibility Wizard** on older antivirus programs, disc utilities, or other system programs, it will create security risks and loss of data.

To open the **Program Compatibility Wizard**, use the **Start**, **Control Panel**, click **Programs** (in **Category View**), and then click the **Use an older program with this version of Windows** link, as shown in Fig. 13.17 to start the Wizard (Fig. 13.18).

Fig. 13.17 The Control Panel Programs Screen.

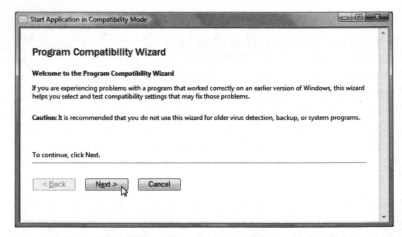

Fig. 13.18 The First Program Compatibility Wizard Screen.

Next, click the **Next** button to display the second Wizard screen, as shown in Fig. 13.19.

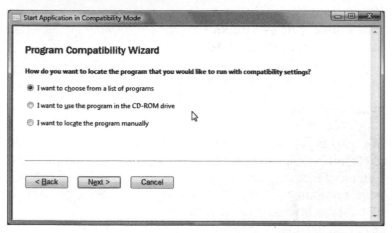

Fig. 13.19 The Second Program Compatibility Wizard Screen.

On this screen, select one of the three options:

* I want to choose from a list of programs
* I want to use the program in the CD-ROM drive
* I want to locate the program manually.

Then click the **Next** button. If you choose the first option, the Wizard will list all the programs on your PC for you to choose the one that misbehaves. From then on, just follow the suggestions of the Wizard. Good luck!

* * *

In Chapter 14 we discus how to look after your PC. We introduce topics such as the Windows Update, the System Restore, and how to clean up and defragment your computer's hard disc. Finally, we conclude with a discussion on backing up your data.

* * *

14

Looking After your PC

Windows Vista comes equipped with a full range of utilities so that you can easily maintain your PC's health. You can access all these tools by using the **Start**, **All Programs**, **Accessories**, and selecting **System Tools**. This opens the menu options shown in Fig. 14.1 below.

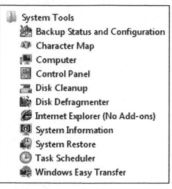

Fig. 14.1 The System Tools Menu.

Of all the available tools, the **System Information** is the easiest to examine – it displays a number of options such as Operating System, System Summary, Hardware Resources, etc. However, as each one of these is bound to be different for different PCs, we leave it to you to examine the information for your system.

Problem Prevention

Windows Vista provides a threefold protection against System corruption. These are:

- System File Protection
- Automatic Update
- System Restore

These will be discussed shortly, so now all you have to look after is your data which can easily be copied to a CD as discussed earlier in the book. After all, hard discs can 'crash' and your PC could be stolen, or lost in a fire, or flood. Any of these events would cause a serious data loss, unless you had a copy of it all, and stored it safely.

System File Protection

Windows applications sometimes can, and do, overwrite important **System** files which, in the past, could render your system unusable. Windows Vista protects such **System** files by automatically restoring them to their original version, if any changes have been attempted by an application program.

Automatic Update

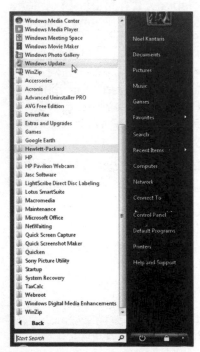

Windows Vista can update automatically any **System** files, if these become available, from Microsoft's Web site. All you have to do is click **Start, All Programs**, and select the **Windows Update** menu option, as shown here in Fig. 14.2.

After connecting to the Internet, your browser will be connected to Microsoft's Web site, as shown in Fig. 14.3 on the next page.

Fig. 14.2 The Windows Update Menu Option.

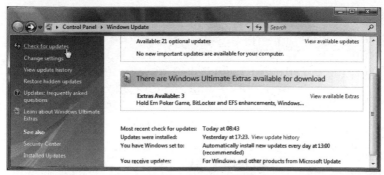

Fig. 14.3 Checking for Updates.

Next, click the **Check for updates** link on the left panel to get a list of updates for your system. The **Update** program returns information of all the available updates which you can see by clicking the **View available updates** link at the top right corner of the screen. There is no point downloading updates that have no relevance to you. For example, almost all of the **Optional updates** returned here are to do with foreign languages.

Finally, click the **Change settings** link (second on the list of links on the left panel) and change the setting to **Download updates but let me choose whether to install them** link. You really need to know what is being installed on your hard disc!

Fig. 14.4 Changing Settings to Microsoft's Update Program.

System Restore

If things go really wrong, **System Restore** can be used to return your PC to the last date it was working perfectly. Every time you start to install a new program, Windows Vista takes a snapshot of your system prior to starting the new installation. Alternatively, you can force Windows to take a snapshot at any time you choose.

To examine the utility, use the **Start, All Programs, Accessories, System Tools** and click on its entry, shown here, which displays the screen in Fig. 14.5.

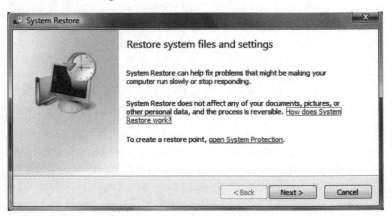

Fig. 14.5 The Welcome to System Restore Screen.

As you can see, from this screen you can select to **Restore** your computer to an earlier time by clicking **Next**, or create a Restore point by clicking the **open System Protection** link.

To demonstrate further what happens, we chose to restore our computer to an earlier time by clicking the **Next** button. This displays a further screen, as shown in Fig. 14.6 on the next page.

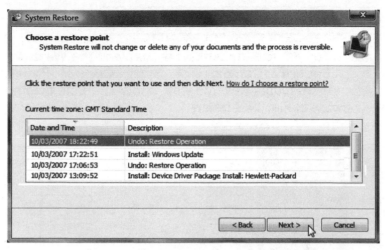

Fig. 14.6 Available System Restore Points.

Selecting a **System Restore** point and clicking **Next**, starts the **Restore** process. Once started you must not stop your computer for any reason whatsoever, otherwise you are running the risk of not being able to start Windows. Just follow the instructions on screen.

If you select to create a **Manual Restore** point, click the **open System Protection** link (see Fig. 14.5 on previous page), to display the screen shown in Fig. 14.7 and click the **Create** button.

Fig. 14.7 A Manual Restore Point.

The Windows Security Center

To examine the options available in the Windows **Security Center**, click **Start**, **Control Panel**, then double-click the icon, shown here, to display the window in Fig. 14.8 below.

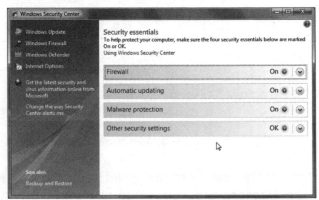

Fig. 14.8 The Windows Security Center.

It is a good idea to switch 'On' the listed items on this screen. The **Firewall** is a software security system that sits between a network and the outside world and is used to set restrictions on what information is communicated from your home or small office network to and from the Internet. It protects you from uninvited outside access.

Switching on the **Automatic updating** option is vital, but make sure you change the setting to **Download updates but let me choose whether to install them** (see page 265).

Malware (malicious software) protection checks your computer to see if you are using up-to-date antispyware and antivirus software. If your antivirus or antispyware software is turned off or out of date, **Security Center** will display a notification and put a **Security Center** ⊗ icon in the notification area.

Disk Cleanup

You can run **Disk Cleanup** to help you free up space on your hard drive. To start the program, use the **Start**, **All Programs**, **Accessories**, **System**  **Tools** command and click the **Disk Cleanup** entry.

The first thing that **Disk Cleanup** does after activation, is to ask you to select which files to clean up, as shown in Fig. 14.9, then asks you which drive you want to clean

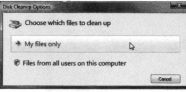

Fig. 14.9 Selecting a Drive.

up. It then scans the specified drive, and then lists temporary files, Internet cache files, and other program files that you can safely delete, as shown in Fig. 14.10 below. **BUT** stop at this point.

Fig. 14.10 Files Found by Cleanup.

As you can see, we could free quite a bit of disc space by deleting all **Temporary Internet Files,** and even more by deleting the **Hibernation File Cleaner**. <u>Do not proceed</u> with the latter delete until you read the small print in Fig. 14.11, which is displayed after highlighting the **Hibernation File Cleaner** entry.

Fig. 14.11 Effect of Deleting the Hibernation File Cleaner.

We strongly suggest you remove the check mark from the **Hibernation File Cleaner** before continuing, because you will lose your ability to **Hibernate** your PC and getting it back is a bit complicated.

Finally, repeat this procedure for both file selection options listed in Fig. 14.9 but DO NOT delete the **Hibernation File Cleane**r, unless you want to.

If it is too late and you have already deleted the **Hibernation File Cleaner**, don't worry, we'll tell you what has taken place and how to get it back.

The reason why hibernation has been disabled is because the Disk Cleanup Wizard has removed the **hiberfil.sys** file from the system, which prevents your computer from hibernating.

To re-enable hibernation, you will need to launch an 'elevated' command prompt, but you must be logged in as 'Administrator'. To do this click the **Start** button, then type in the **Start Search** box the command **cmd** and press the **Enter** key. This opens the **Command Prompt** as shown in Fig. 14.12 below with the Administrator's user name on the first line.

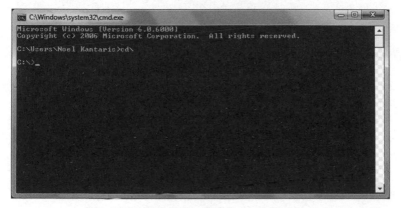

Fig. 14.12 The Command Prompt Screen.

Next type **CD** and press the **Enter** key which displays what appears on the second line, namely **C:\>** with the pulsing cursor waiting for you to type a command. Now type the command '**powercfg -h on**' without the quotes, but with the spaces as shown, and press the **Enter** key. This should re-enable hibernation by recreating the **hiberfil.sys** file. You should restart your computer to see the hibernate options.

Defragmenting your Hard Discs

The **Disk Defragmenter** optimises a hard disc by rearranging the data on it to eliminate unused spaces, which speeds up access to the disc by Windows operations. You don't need to exit a running application before starting **Disk Defragmenter**.

To start the program use the **Start**, **All Programs**, **Accessories**, **System Tools** and select the **Disk Defragmenter** entry. Next, choose which drive you want to defragment and click the **Defragment Now** button to display a screen similar to that in Fig. 14.13.

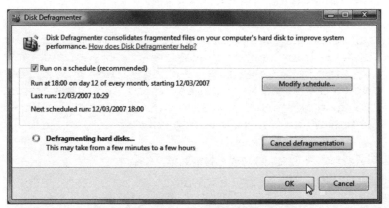

Fig. 14.13 Defragmentation in Progress.

You can defragment a drive in the background while working by minimising the utility onto the **Taskbar**. In Windows Vista you cannot waste your time by watching a graphical representation of the operation on screen, unless you like watching a small circle going around and around for a few hours! In fact, you get no messages at all from the defragmenter, not even when it finishes the process, except for the focus on the default button changing from **Cancel defragmentation** to ✅ .

Backing up your Data

Hard discs can 'crash' (though not as often these days as they used to) or your PC could be stolen, or lost in a fire or flood. Any of these events would cause a serious data loss, unless you had backed up all your data on a regular basis, and stored it somewhere safely, preferably away from the vicinity of your PC.

Although Microsoft includes with Windows Vista Business and Ultimate editions a **Backup** program, we will not discuss it here but will suggest an alternative procedure. After all, users of Windows Vista Home Edition (both Basic and Premium) have just as important data that needs to be backed up!

On the last section of this chapter we discuss a method of backing up your whole computer, including the Windows Vista operating system plus all your programs and their settings and all your data. This is by far our preferred method as it is easy to do, but costs around £75 to implement. But first, let us discuss the cheaper method of backing up your data only.

Making a Back-up of your Data

The destination for the back-up could be an external hard disc, a zip drive, or a CD/DVD recorder. In the latter case, you will need a rewritable compact disc (CD-RW) or a rewritable DVD (DVD-RW). Since these days most users have a computer with a CD rewriter, we will use this as the back-up destination in our example, although you can apply the procedure to any of the other media mentioned above.

To start the back-up process, insert a blank rewritable CD or DVD in the CD/DVD recorder (or whatever other media you have chosen for your back-up into an appropriate drive or USB port), then do the following:

- Use the **Start**, **Computer** menu option to locate and select the files or folders you want to back up. These are most likely to be found in the **Documents**, **Pictures**, **Music**, and **Games** folders of a user.

- Whether you select to back up the entire folders mentioned here, will depend on the capacity of your backing-up media.

- If the contents of your major folders are larger in size than your backing-up media, then decide which sub-folders or files you want to back up.

- While selecting such sub-folders or files, keep the **Ctrl** key depressed, if they are not contiguous on the displayed list. In our example in Fig. 14.14 below, we chose to back up the five highlighted folders on our D: drive.

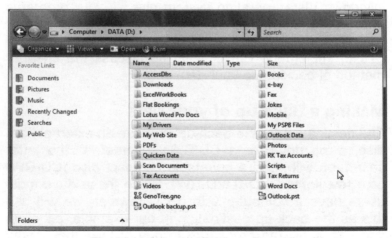

Fig. 14.14 Selecting Folder to Back Up.

- Next, and while these sub-folders or files are selected and the **Ctrl** key is still depressed, right-click near your selection, and on the displayed menu choose the **Properties** option.

We do this in order to find out the size of the selected items, as shown in Fig. 10.15 below.

Fig. 14.15 The Size of Selected Items.

As you can see, the selected folders require 143 MB of disc space and, naturally, will fit on either a 650 MB CD or a 4.7 GB DVD. Therefore, it might be a good idea if you increase your selection.

You could also compress each folder in turn by right-clicking it, and choosing the **Send To**, **Compressed (zipped) Folder** option from the drop-down menu. In that case, you might find that you can fit an even larger number of zipped folders on one CD. Whether you choose to compress these folders or not, before making the back-up, is a matter of personal choice.

For this example, we will first proceed with our selection, then we are going to back up the five folders onto one CD-RW, but if you do have a DVD rewriter, then you can select a much larger number of folders to back up.

To continue with the back-up process, do the following:

- Select the folders that will fit on one CD or DVD (or your chosen back-up media).

- While still holding the **Ctrl** key depressed, right-click near your selection and choose the **Send To** option, then click the back-up destination drive – drive E: in our case, as shown in Fig. 14.16.

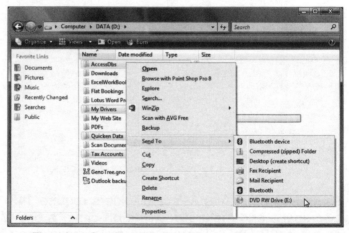

Fig. 14.16 Sending Selected Items to Back-up Media.

If this is the first time you are using a CD or DVD disc, it will be formatted before the copying process begins. The selected folders are then copied to memory, before they are written to disc. For our selection of folders it took about twenty minutes to complete the back-up process.

In reality we tend to use an external portable USB disc drive for backing up complete data folders. In our case we can back up 5.1 GB in just seven minutes!

Retrieving Back-up Files

Once the writing process is finished, examine the contents of your back-up media. You should find a complete duplicate of all the selected files and folders as shown in Fig. 14.17 below.

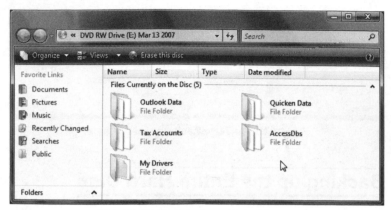

Fig. 14.17 The Back-up List of Items.

To restore data from the back-up media, copy it back to the place it first came from. In our example this is the D: drive.

Adding Files and Folders to a Back-up

To add files and folders to a back-up, select the required files or folder and send it to the back-up drive. This will only succeed provided the addition of these files or folder to the existing back-up does not cause it to exceed the capacity of the media.

In Fig. 14.18, we show the contents of our CD disc, after adding to it three more folders, namely, ExcelWorkBooks, My Web Site, and PDFs from our D: drive, a total of 28.6 MB which took less than four minutes to copy.

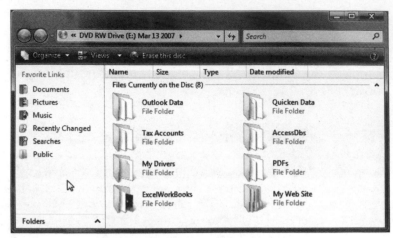

Fig. 14.18 The New Back-up List of Items.

Backing up the Entire Hard Disc

If your computer is running Windows Vista Ultimate or Vista Business, then you already have the software required to make an image of your entire drive, including the operating system. Just follow the trail **Start**, **Control Panel**, click on the **Welcome Centre**, click the link **Show all 14 items**, then click the **Back up and Restore Center** icon, and follow the instructions on screen.

Users of Windows Vista Home version (the majority of Vista users in our opinion) can buy a program which can do everything that is required to make a an image of their hard drive. Although 'Norton Ghost' is well known, we feel that the best solution today is 'Acronis True Image 10 Home' for around £25 (www.acronis.com).

True Image 10 supports both Windows XP and Windows Vista, allowing you to make a clone of your hard drive which, in the event of disc failure or PC theft, can be used to restore your entire set-up.

You will, however, be wise to buy an external USB pocket size hard drive (for around £50 for 100 GB), and store the image of your hard drive on it. This allows you to keep the back-up away from the vicinity of your PC, thus increasing security.

True Image allows you to make complete, and incremental back-up sets and also lets you browse your back-ups and restore individual file, folders, or the entire Operating System with all your programs and their settings. In fact, we will go as far as to say that we will not be without it! Compare the 40 minutes it takes to recover the complete system to the days it will take you to install Windows from scratch, then all the programs you use, then all your data ... unthinkable!

We hope we have convinced you how easy it is and how necessary to make regular back-ups of your important data. Believe us, there is nothing more devastating than losing all your letters, pictures, videos, and all the other items you treasure so much for the sake of spending half an hour or so every week. Good luck!

* * *

There is a lot more to Windows Vista than what we have covered in this book – but we have to stop somewhere and this is as good a point as any! We hope we have covered enough topics and in sufficient depth for you to feel confident enough to forge on by yourselves.

* * *

15

Glossary of Terms

Access control	A security mechanism that determines which operations a user is authorised to perform on a PC, a file, a printer, etc.
Active	Describes the folder, window or icon that you are currently using or that is currently selected.
Add-in	A mini-program which runs in conjunction with another and enhances its functionality.
ActiveX	A set of technologies that enables software components to interact with one another in a network, regardless of the language of their creation.
Address	A unique number or name that identifies a specific computer or user on a network.
Administrator	The person responsible for setting up and managing local computers, their user and group accounts, and assigning passwords and permissions.
Applet	A program that can be downloaded over a network and launched on the user's computer.

Association	An identification of a filename extension to a program. This lets Windows open the program when its files are selected.
AVI	Audio Video Interleaved. A Windows multimedia file format for sound and moving pictures.
Background	The screen background image used on a graphical user interface such as Windows.
Backup	To make a back-up copy of a file or a disc for safekeeping.
Bandwidth	The range of transmission frequencies a network can use. The greater the bandwidth the more information that can be transferred over a network.
Baud rate	The speed at which a modem communicates.
Bit	The smallest unit of information handled by a computer.
Bookmark	A marker inserted at a specific point in a document. Used as a target for a hypertext link, or to enable a user to return for later reference.
Boot up	To start your PC by switching it on, which initiates a self-test of its RAM, then loads the necessary system files.
Byte	A unit of data that holds a single character, such as a letter, or a digit.
Cache	An area of memory, or disc space, reserved for data, which speeds up downloading.

CD-R	Recordable compact disc.
CD-ROM	Read Only Memory compact disc. Data can be read but not written.
CD-RW	Rewritable compact disc. Data can be copied to the CD on more than one occasion and can be erased.
Client	A PC that has access to services over a computer network. The computer providing the services is a server.
Clipboard	A temporary storage area of memory, where text and graphics are stored with the Windows cut and copy actions.
Command	An instruction given to a computer to carry out a particular action.
Compressed file	One that is compacted to save server space and reduce transfer times. In Windows the file extension is .zip.
Configuration	A general term referring to the way you have your computer set up.
Context menu	A menu that opens when you right-click the mouse button on a feature.
Cookies	Files stored on your hard drive by your Web browser that hold information for it to use.
CPU	The Central Processing Unit. The main chip that executes all instructions entered into a computer.
Default	The command, device or option automatically chosen.
Device driver	A special file that must be loaded into memory for Windows to be able to

address a specific procedure or hardware device.

Device name   A logical name used to identify a device, such as LPT1 or COM1 for the parallel or serial printer.

Digital signature A means for originators of a message, file, or other digitally encoded information to bind their identity to the information.

Domain   A group of devices, servers and computers on a network.

Domain Name   The name of an Internet site, for example www.microsoft.com.

Download   The process of transferring files between PCs or the Internet and a PC.

Drag   To move an object on the screen by pressing and holding down the left mouse button while moving the mouse.

Drive name   The letter followed by a colon which identifies a floppy or hard disc drive.

DSL   Digital Subscriber Line. A broadband connection to the Internet through existing copper telephone wires.

Engine   Software used by search services.

Ethernet   A very common method of networking computers in a LAN.

Extract a file   Create an uncompressed copy of the file in a folder you specify.

File extension   The suffix following the period in a filename. Windows uses this to identify the source application program. For example .jpg indicates a graphic file.

Firewall	Security measures designed to protect a networked system, or a PC, from unauthorised access.
Format	The structure of a file that defines the way it is stored and laid out on the screen or in print.
Fragmentation	The scattering of parts of the same file over different areas of the disc.
FTP	File Transfer Protocol. The procedure for connecting to a remote computer and transferring files.
Function key	One of the series of 10 or 12 keys marked with the letter F and a numeral, used for specific operations.
Gigabyte	(GB); 1,024 megabytes. Usually thought of as one billion bytes.
Graphic	A picture or illustration, also called an image. Formats include GIF, JPEG, BMP, PCX, and TIFF.
Group	A collection of users, computers, contacts, and other groups.
Hardware	The equipment that makes up a computer system, excluding the programs or software.
Hibernation	A state in which your computer shuts down after saving everything in memory on your hard disc.

Home page	The document displayed when you first open your Web browser, or the first document you come to at a Web site.
Host	Computer connected directly to the Internet that provides services to other local and/or remote computers.
HTTP	HyperText Transport Protocol. The system used to link and transfer hypertext documents on the Web.
Hub	A common connection point for devices in a network.
Hyperlink	A segment of text, or an image, that refers to another document on the Web, an intranet or your PC.
Hypermedia	Hypertext extended to include linked multimedia.
Hypertext	A system that allows documents to be cross-linked so that the reader can explore related links, or documents, by clicking on a highlighted symbol.
Interface	A device that allows you to connect a computer to its peripherals.
Internet	The global system of computer networks.
Intranet	A private network inside an organisation using the same kind of software as the Internet.
IP	Internet Protocol. The rules that provide basic Internet functions.

IP Address	Internet Protocol Address. Every PC on the Internet has a unique identifying number.
ISDN	Integrated Services Digital Network, a telecom standard using digital transmission technology to support voice, video and data communications applications over regular telephone lines.
ISP	Internet Service Provider. A company that offers access to the Internet.
JPEG / JPG	Joint Photographic Experts Group, a popular cross-platform format for image files. JPEG is best suited for true colour original images.
Kilobyte	(KB); 1024 bytes of information or storage space.
LAN	Local Area Network. A high-speed network in an office or a building.
Linked object	An object that is inserted into a document but still exists in the source file. Changing the original object automatically updates it within the linked document.
Links	The hypertext connections between Web pages.
Local	A resource that is located on your computer, not linked to it over a network.
Location	An Internet address.
Log on	To gain access to a network, or the Internet.

Malware	Generic term for software designed to perform harmful or surreptitious acts.
Megabyte	(MB); 1024 kilobytes of information or storage space.
Megahertz	(MHz); Speed of processor in millions of cycles per second.
MIDI	Musical Instrument Digital Interface. Allows devices to transmit and receive sound and music.
MIME	Multipurpose Internet Mail Extensions, a messaging standard that allows Internet users to exchange e-mail messages enhanced with graphics, video and voice.
Modem	Short for Modulator-demodulator. An electronic device that lets PCs communicate electronically.
Multimedia	The use of photographs, music and sound and movie images in a presentation.
Multitasking	Performing more than one operation at the same time.
Network	Two or more computers connected together to share resources.
Network server	Central computer which stores files for several linked computers.
Node	Any single computer connected to a network.
NTFS file	An advanced file system that provides performance, security, and reliability.

OLE	Object Linking and Embedding. A technology for transferring and sharing information between software applications.
Page	An HTML document, or Web site.
Parallel port	The input/output connector for a parallel interface device. Printers are normally plugged into a parallel port.
Partition	A portion of a physical disc that functions as though it were a physically separate disc.
PATH	The location of a file in the directory tree.
PDF	Portable Document Format. A file format developed by Adobe that allows formatted pages of text and graphics to be viewed and printed correctly on any computer with a PDF Reader.
Peripheral	Any device attached to a PC.
Pixel	The smallest picture element on screen that can be independently assigned colour and intensity.
Plug-and-play	Hardware which can be plugged into a PC and be used immediately without configuration.
POP	Post Office Protocol. A method of storing and returning e-mail.
Port	The place where information goes into or out of a computer, such as a modem.

PostScript	A page-description language (PDL), developed by Adobe Systems for printing on laser printers.
Protocol	A set of rules or standards that define how computers communicate with each other.
Queue	A list of e-mail messages waiting to be sent over the Internet, or files to a printer.
RAM	Random Access Memory; the PC's volatile memory. Data held in it is lost when power is switched off.
Registry	A database where information about a PC's configuration is deposited. The registry contains information that Windows continually references during its operation.
Remote PC	A PC that you can access only via a communications device, such as a modem, or a communications line.
Resource	A directory, or printer, that can be shared over a network.
Robot	A Web agent that visits sites, by requesting documents from them, for the purposes of indexing for search engines. Also known as Wanderers, Crawlers, or Spiders.
ROM	Read Only Memory; a PC's non-volatile memory. Data is written into this memory at manufacture and is not affected by power loss.
RTF	Rich Text Format. A common file format used to transfer files between different

programs. It preserves most of the formatting of a document.

Screen saver   A moving picture or pattern that appears on your screen when you have not used the mouse or keyboard for a specified period of time.

Script   A type of program consisting of a set of instructions to an application or tool program.

Search engine   A program that helps users find information across the Internet.

Server   A computer system that manages and delivers information for client computers.

Shared resource Any device, program or file that is available to network users.

Site   A place on the Internet. Every Web page has a location where it resides which is called its site.

Sleep   A state in which your computer consumes less power when it is idle, but remains available for immediate use.

SMTP   Simple Mail Transfer Protocol. A protocol dictating how e-mail messages are exchanged over the Internet.

Software   The programs and instructions that control your PC.

Spamming   Sending the same message to a large number of mailing lists or newsgroups.

Spider   See robot.

Spooler	Software which handles the transfer of information to a store to be used by a peripheral device.
SVGA	Super Video Graphics Array.
Swap file	An area of your hard disc, also known as virtual memory, used to store temporary operating files
System disc	A disc containing files to enable a PC to start up.
System files	Files used by a PC to load, configure, and run the operating system.
Task Manager	A utility that provides information about programs and processes running on the computer.
Uninstall	To remove an application from your hard disc and related registry data.
Upload	The process of transferring files between PCs or a PC and the Internet.
URL	Uniform Resource Locator, the addressing system used on the Web.
USB	Universal Serial Bus. An external bus standard that enables data transfer rates of 12 Mbps.
Virus	A malicious program, downloaded from a web site or disc, designed to wipe out information on your PC.
Wizard	A Microsoft tool that steps you through certain operations, or asks you questions and then creates an object depending on your answers.

Index